Misfits & Me

MANDY SAYER won the Vogel Award with her first novel, *Mood Indigo*. Since then she has published five works of fiction and six works of non-fiction, including the memoirs *Dreamtime Alice*, winner of the National Biography Award; *Velocity*, winner of the Age Book of the Year for Non-Fiction and the South Australian Premier's Award for Non-Fiction; and *The Poet's Wife*, shortlisted for the West Australian Premier's Award. Her study of Romani culture, *Australian Gypsies: Their secret history*, was published to acclaim in 2017. She lives in Sydney with her husband, playwright and author, Louis Nowra, and their dogs, Coco and Basil.

mandysayer.com.au

Also by Mandy Sayer

FICTION
Love in the Years of Lunacy
The Night has a Thousand Eyes
Fifteen Kinds of Desire
The Cross
Blind Luck
Mood Indigo

NON-FICTION
Australian Gypsies: Their secret history
The Poet's Wife: A memoir of a marriage
Velocity: A memoir
Dreamtime Alice: A memoir
Coco: Autobiography of my dog

OTHER
The Australian Long Story, ed.
In the Gutter … Looking at the Stars, ed. with Louis Nowra

COLLECTED NON-FICTION

Mandy Sayer
Misfits & Me

NEWSOUTH

A NewSouth book

Published by
NewSouth Publishing
University of New South Wales Press Ltd
University of New South Wales
Sydney NSW 2052
AUSTRALIA
newsouthpublishing.com

 A catalogue record for this
book is available from the
National Library of Australia

ISBN   9781742236100 (paperback)
            9781742244334 (ebook)
            9781742248769 (ePDF)

Design Josephine Pajor-Markus
Cover design Nada Backovic
Cover image Adam Knott

To Louis, my favourite misfit

Contents

Prelude *ix*

LIFE *1*

People Power at Ponderosa *3*

Wild Frontier: The Child Gangs of Tweed Heads *18*

The Hordes *37*

The Tincture of Health *40*

Flying High: The Rise and Guise of Self-Funded Retirees *45*

Girls Gone Wild *57*

Elsie Turns Forty *70*

LOVE *83*

Love and Death in Darlinghurst *85*

My New Orleans *105*

Sleepless in Samoa *113*

A Writer in the Family *124*

For the Love of Dog *128*

The Gift of Life *137*

Goodbye, Pork Pie Hat: Fourteen Ways to Say Farewell *149*

LITERATURE AND ART *163*

Thea Astley Comes Out of the Shadows *165*

Sex, Lies and Defamation *178*

In Ernest: Hemingway and the Art of the Story *188*

Satirists of Suburbia: Mrs Edna Everage Paints John Brack *201*

Letter to a Young Novelist *208*

Shaun Prescott: Modern Misfit *224*

CODA *231*

ACKNOWLEDGMENTS *241*

Prelude

I fell in love with my first misfit at the age of three. He was a disabled man in a wheelchair who sold newspapers every afternoon outside the Empire Hotel in Annandale, Sydney. Whenever I glimpsed him in the distance I would break into a run, jump onto his lap and smother him with kisses. I nicknamed him 'Lurch', after a television character I also loved, the tall, taciturn butler on *The Addams Family*. In my mind, the two men were one, and whenever Lurch the butler exited a scene on the screen, I would hang out the living room window and strain to see him on the street. Misfits have intrigued me ever since.

Misfits often have a history of trying to fit into the dominant culture, but to an extent have failed or have grown disillusioned. As a child, my father spent the first seven years of his life in hospital, enduring scores of primitive surgeries to mend his cleft lip and cleft palate, and had no formal education (or socialisation) until his release. His concerned parents placed him in a private school, where he was later warned by the principal that if he didn't play football, he wouldn't be able to mix in general society. Already, at the age of nine, he'd given up trying to assimilate into 'general society', preferring instead the solitary study of music. My husband Louis, who at the age of twelve suffered a near-fatal head accident and had to learn to speak again, has often told that when he was a young man he just 'wanted to be normal', and would study the gestures and habits of other people so as to appear to be one of them.

Exclusion from society can at times be painful, but under the right circumstances it can also become a form of freedom. The disenfranchised create small niches of power wherever and whenever they can – and it is within these niches that they exercise imagination, resilience and creativity. For example, I have two elderly cousins – brother and sister – who have lived together for decades in their late mother's art deco house (see 'The Hordes'). They have also inherited their mother's obsession with hoarding, so much so that they use a Kookaburra stove as a dispensary, and stacks of old newspapers for shelving. Another example would be Don Miller, featured in the essay 'Flying High', a gifted elderly chemist who would rather cook meth for a Lebanese bikie gang than run his own business, because it satisfied his boundless curiosity. Misfits find ways to take advantage of their outsider status to make more meaningful lives for themselves and others. Misfits don't undermine the status quo; they tend to ignore it.

From my experience, misfits are devoid of self-pity and are usually quite inventive. My younger brother, for example, used to take two breaks a day from his job as a housepainter to perform dialysis on himself with a portable machine in the back seat of his car (further discussed in 'The Gift of Life'). Another example would be Aboriginal Elder Tony Bower, who drives around NSW in a mobile marijuana dispensary, giving away cannabis oil tinctures that he makes himself to sufferers of cancer, multiple sclerosis, depression, diabetes – all the while risking arrest and jail. In 'The Tincture of Health', he claims, 'I've explained to the government and the cops that I am Aboriginal and it is against my culture to refuse help or comfort to someone in need'.

Misfits usually have no choice but to live within the fissures of modern society, where they largely remain unnoticed and invisible, unless one of them breaks the law too many times. Some, but not all, are damaged – either physically, emotionally, or psychologically – and find unique ways of coping with their difference.

Occasionally, an outsider status can be conferred on a town or a particular area – and unofficially becomes a geographical misfit. The various settings that are referenced in this collection certainly earn this moniker. Darlinghurst and Kings Cross embody tales of transitory lives – transgressive writers and transvestite shop keepers; Apia, Samoa, features feral dogs, serial killers, dengue fever and local standover men; New Orleans tells true stories of professional warlocks, tap dancing street kids, and of a city that has the longest social calendar yet shortest lifespan in America.

Misfits are not self-consciously unusual, or deliberately trying to be 'different'. Due to the accidents of birth, class, genetic inheritance and environment, they often have no choice: both nature and nurture conspire to spawn a genuine outsider. My feature-length profile on Nick Cave, for example, did not make the cut for this collection. Sure, Cave is talented, innovative and individual, but any transgressive or 'misfitting' behaviour is likely to be self-conscious and is enacted to polish his bad-boy persona. True misfits rarely worry about reputation or material reward, and tend to live in the present moment.

Moreover, in my experience, creative misfits have little regard for fame, riches or their 'artistic legacy', but are consumed instead with merely perfecting the book, the composition or the painting they're currently working on, which is discussed at length in 'Letter to a Young Novelist' and in the final essay, 'Shaun Prescott: Modern Misfit'. Although he does not appear in this book, Ian Fairweather is a fine example of my definition of a creative misfit: content to live out his last years alone in a hut on Bribie Island, while continuing to paint daily his distinctive landscapes. Painter John Brack, who is discussed in 'Satirists of Suburbia', toiled away in obscurity for forty years, and was forced to earn his living by teaching art at the National Gallery. In the 1980s, when his paintings finally began selling for high prices after decades of commercial failure, he began to panic. At the time he confessed that, 'If I'm going to be so popular,

I feel uneasy, so I must paint a picture that is A) unpopular and B) unsaleable'.

Typically, misfits don't play by the rules, but tend to create their own ones. Teenage carjackers Jamie and Leeyah, for example, featured in 'Girls Gone Wild', once told me that they don't just rob anyone: 'Like, we wouldn't have stolen the car if there'd been a baby in the back, or if it'd been an old person driving … We do have ethics, you know!' Similarly, the elderly people referenced in 'Flying High', who supplement their old-age pensions by dealing drugs, all told me individually that their one rule is that they never sell to minors.

Many misfits are loners at heart, but if they are lucky enough to find a kindred spirit or community, they end up treasuring it. The neighbours living in a Sydney Public Housing block, discussed in 'People Power at Ponderosa', are classic examples of misfits curating a supportive and family-like community with very few resources and no support from the outside world. And misfits know how to improvise with and adapt to situations that would leave a non-misfit paralysed: these same neighbours deal with a junkie resident who runs his noisy washing machine day and night by breaking into the building's switch box and turning the junkie's electricity off.

'Eccentric', 'Bohemian' and 'off-beat' are adjectives that insiders always use to describe outsiders. The modifiers usually contain a pejorative subtext: it's not so much a fear of 'the other', but a dismissal of 'the other', and much of this indifference is based on class. A few years ago, when I was struggling financially, a publisher gave me some unsolicited advice: 'If you want to be successful, write a novel about the middle-aged and the middle class.' Even today, somehow the experiences of the advantaged in our culture are perceived to be more significant than those of the welfare and working classes.

Coverage of the #MeToo movement is a case in point: in Australia, more than one woman a week is murdered by her husband or partner, but news outlets and social media are much more concerned with the comparatively minor problems of rich and famous actresses. Frankly, I don't care if a musical theatre performer flashed a woman backstage, or if an actor followed his co-star into the bathroom. I care about a young friend called Polly, who, while suffering post-natal internal injuries that required the use of a colostomy bag, was raped repeatedly by the sadistic father of her newborn child. Or my friend, Marie, who was bashed every day by her husband for twenty-two years. Or the 714 cases of sexual offence involving children under the age of sixteen during the past five years in the Northern Territory. Where are the hashtags acknowledging them?

***

I find myself drawn to misfits because I have felt like an outsider for most of my life. By the age of fourteen, I'd endured severe domestic violence, homelessness, sexual abuse at the hands of a teacher and my stepfather, and had attended twelve public schools throughout three states. Every time I began a new school, to avoid being bullied, I had to suppress my background and create a public persona, one that concurred with the kinds of kids with whom I had to keep company. When that didn't work I would hide in the library. Any nascent friendships would wither, because some drama in my home life would see my family packing up and moving yet again. In short, I became an unwitting loner, trying in vain to fit in to each subsequent situation, whether it be a new school, another homeless shelter, or the couch of my mother's latest boyfriend.

As a teenager, I learned to tap dance and escaped into the thrilling, nomadic world of street performers, and later travelled throughout the US as part of a double act with my jazz drummer father. Upon entering Indiana University, however, I became a loner again, finding myself the only 25-year-old freshman, and the only Australian, in a class of Midwestern American high school graduates. At the time I was living in a small town, with my African-American husband, only twenty miles away from the national headquarters of the Ku Klux Klan.

It has only occurred to me recently that I am a wife who's never had children, a traveller who's never learned to drive, and an academic who's never held a permanent university position. The only time I feel truly comfortable is when I'm in the company of other outsiders. Misfits amuse me, provoke me and make me feel secure.

Or, to mangle a well-known saying: 'Mis(fit)ery loves company.'

LIFE

People Power at Ponderosa

(2017)

'You know how we can tell that someone has died?' asks Woolley, standing in the corridor of his Public Housing building. He nods at the door of the apartment adjacent to his own unit. 'Flies on the door handle. The flies always figure it out before the smell gets going'. Woolley tells me that last week he noticed the insects buzzing around his neighbour's lock and called the police, who broke in to the flat to discover the corpse of Peter, in his early fifties, who hadn't been seen for three days.

'He was a bit of a conspiracy theorist', adds Woolley, the unofficial caretaker of the building. 'He reckoned JFK was murdered by the Mob'.

Woolley, however, suspects no foul play in the death of his neighbour. Now there is a sign on the door, posted by the authorities, warning that the interior has been contaminated and that no one should enter until it has been detoxified by forensic cleaners.

'Probably an overdose', he murmurs.

Residents call the building 'Ponderosa', in reference to the ranch on long-running US TV western *Bonanza*. It's a block of twenty-four studio apartments in Sydney's eastern suburbs, built in the 1970s, filled with single disability and aged pensioners. All but one survive on Centrelink payments and donations from charities. The majority, Woolley tells me, have no family support.

3

It's now ten days until Christmas, but he is ambivalent about organising the annual party because four of the building's residents are in hospital and the recent passing of his neighbour puts Ponderosa's death toll for the year at three (thus far). 'You don't want to plan Christmas too far ahead, because you don't know who's going to die between now and then'.

Woolley leads me into his studio filled with clothing racks and his collection of vintage Hawaiian shirts. A three-quarter bed is wedged into an alcove. A flat-screen TV is mounted on the wall, below a small round table. It's a tight squeeze, even for one person. I ask him about the actual size of the unit. He shrugs and replies, 'Nine paces by five paces. That's how I measure it'.

We walk out into his small, private courtyard and he shows me a huge freezer he's installed under the awning, where anyone in the building is welcome to store their frozen goods. In order to provide round-the-clock access, Woolley has removed three palings from his fence so his neighbours can duck in and out without disturbing him.

As we walk back inside, 84-year-old Don, who lives upstairs, limps through the open door carrying a steaming plate of fish and chips. He delivers it to the kitchen counter. Don is the unofficial chef for six other Ponderosa dwellers who are either too ill or too lazy to cook a hot meal at night.

'Sunday is a baked dinner', Don says, leaning against the wall and lighting a cigarette. 'Wednesday is spaghetti bolognaise, or lasagne. And Friday is fish and chips'.

'Three good square meals a week', adds Woolley. 'That's enough to keep us going'.

Every Friday morning, Don gets up, collects his shopping trolley and limps fifteen minutes to the local outlet of the charity OzHarvest, where he selects donated fruits and vegetables for his various neighbours. 'I know that Jose likes Asian greens. And Butch loves kiwifruit. I know what everyone wants so I can pick up stuff for them'.

'And on Fridays we do the washing up and return the plates to Don', adds Woolley. 'And we check his fridge to see what he needs'.

'Do you charge people for the meals?' I ask.

Don smiles and glances at Woolley.

'We've got a kind of bartering system', says Woolley. 'It's all based on reciprocity'.

He tells me that some years ago the residents of Ponderosa worked out a plan that would benefit them all – and one that would remove the need to constantly borrow and repay money to each other. 'For example, we all buy the same cask wine – Golden Oak, $12 for 4 litres from the cellars down the road'.

'Sometimes it's $10', chimes in Don. 'When it's on special'.

'We all smoke the same tobacco – "Endless Blue" – and use the same papers, "Tally-Hos"'.

'It's an open-door policy … ' adds Don, stubbing out his cigarette.

I glance at Woolley, hoping he'll further explain the scheme. '… so we can walk in and out of each other's apartments. Say if I run out of wine, I can stroll into someone else's place and help myself. Same with tobacco. And food. And they can let themselves in to my place, without having to find me'. The ninety-year-olds are housed on the second floor, so they have level access to street exits. Woolley also tells me that all the men in the building have swapped three sets of keys, so that no one is accidentally locked out of his unit.

'And when one of us goes to hospital', he adds, 'the rest of us sneak into the empty apartment and clean it all up – like a bunch of elves!'

Sixteen years ago, when Woolley and Don first moved in, the side garden was denuded and filled with trash. Drug dealers stalked the security gates. When Woolley called the police, he was referred to Public Housing, and when he called the department he was always referred back to the police. So Woolley and his neighbours decided to take matters into their own hands, marshalling sentries at the windows above the security gates. Whenever a dealer was spotted lurking outside, he'd be pelted with rocks and buckets of water. After a month or so, the block was free of both junkies and dealers.

It was then that Woolley, Don and their new friends set about turning the building's common property into a sanctuary. They cleared the garden, planted trees and ferns, and set up tables and chairs in the shade. Now, it exudes the cool green light of a tropical rainforest.

'There's a Chinese guy upstairs', says Woolley. 'He's eighty-six – and we call him Jose'.

'Why do you call him Jose?'

Woolley grins and lights a rollie. ''Cause he's always hosing the garden. We've sort of given him permission to use a fire hose on the third floor. He stands in the corridor and waters the plants from there. You see, we're only supposed to use the hose in the event of a fire. But because Jose is Chinese, we figure that if he ever got into trouble from the authorities he could pretend that he doesn't speak English'.

As Don bids goodbye and disappears into the corridor, Woolley sprinkles his hot dinner with water and pops it into the oven on low.

At night, Ponderosa becomes an amplifier for the many frustrations of the neighbourhood. A guy upstairs has been yelling obscenities over his balcony for five hours. Woolley tells me that he and a neighbour have been warring for days, but no one can remember how it started exactly. Bottles and glasses shatter on the street; car alarms wail; and, just before midnight, I can hear somebody spewing. Soon, police sirens are howling over the shouts of neighbours.

'Raid', says Woolley, calmly, topping up his drink. 'The house two doors up – they're always getting busted'.

Nine Days Until Christmas

The front door swings open. 'You there, Woolley?' cries a man in an urgent voice. 'Woolley, are you there?'

I look up to see a solid, dark-haired man, wearing sunglasses, peering down at me, sporting a wide, maniacal grin.

Woolley rises from his chair and introduces me to Leo, who, at the age of forty-eight, is the 'baby' of the building. They've been close friends since Leo moved in to Ponderosa fifteen years ago. Every morning, he arrives at Woolley's the same time – nine-thirty – and they walk around to a local pub to buy takeaway coffees.

Today is no different. Woolley grabs his mobile phone and they disappear out the door together. I stay behind to await the arrival of a health inspector. Woolley has told me that five units have been badly affected by mould and has already shown me a photograph on his phone of an 87-year-old man slumped on a bed, with the wall behind him furred with mildew.

'Maybe we can paint over it', says Woolley, as he and Leo return with the coffees.

'You can't paint over mould', I say. 'It'll make it even worse'.

'Well, it'll look a lot better', Woolley reasons. 'You know, some of these blokes don't have much time'.

We wait for the health inspector. Leo, who is on the autism spectrum, tells me a little of his life. He was born in Australia to Italian parents who returned to Naples when he was two years old. He grew up speaking fluent Italian. When he was eleven, however, his family moved back to Australia and Leo struggled to adapt both culturally and linguistically. Hence, when he speaks English, he is compelled to state everything twice.

'When he speaks Italian', says Woolley, 'he only says things once'.

Leo does his bit for the Ponderosa community by repairing second-hand mobile phones and giving them to neighbours.

'Everyone gets a basic Nokia when they move in', explains

Woolley. 'And we get them all on the same plan. Thirty bucks a month. It's cheaper than a landline'.

Suddenly, what looks like water or weak tea begins falling past the open door and into the courtyard. It continues for eight or ten seconds and stops as abruptly as it began.

'When we get junkies in here', announces Leo, 'it wrecks everything'. After repeating the statement, Leo lets Woolley pick up the story.

'Since Junkie John moved in two months ago, the cops have been called twice and Bikie Dan, who lives upstairs, has stabbed him once'. Woolley sips his coffee slowly and lights up a rollie.

'Was that just someone pissing over the balcony?' I ask.

Woolley replies by rolling his eyes and shrugging. He goes on to explain that Junkie John supports his habit by stealing luggage from the carousels at Sydney airport. 'The only problem', he continues, 'is that John's a clean freak. As soon as he moved in, he ripped up the carpet of his unit and dumped it in the garden. And he had his own washer and dryer in his unit going 24/7, laundering all the stolen clothes and luggage before he sold them on'.

Leo chimes in – twice – that John also threw his television from his balcony and damaged the herbs that Jose had planted. And one day, a neighbour grew so tired of the noise of the washer and dryer, he got up in the middle of the night, broke in to the power box and secretly turned the junkie's electricity off. So the junkie moved in to the communal laundry, sleeping there and monopolising the three available washing machines.

'And he lives off eggs boiled in an electric jug!' adds Woolley, shaking his head.

We hear footsteps outside and turn towards the open door, anticipating the health inspector. But it's only a neighbour on his way upstairs.

'So how else do you cope', I ask, 'when you're living on such a tight budget?'

'Lowes!' announces Leo enthusiastically. 'Lowes!'

Woolley tells me that all the male residents of Ponderosa have secured a loyalty card from Lowes department store. 'During sales, it's 15 per cent off. You can get a whole new wardrobe for seventy bucks!'

'Tell her about the toilet paper!' enthuses Leo. 'Tell her about the toilet paper!'

Woolley laughs and explains to me that a few years ago, several residents of the building used to raid the expensive restaurants and bars in the area and steal rolls of high-quality Sorbent. They would then meet at a local pub with their bounties and pretend it was an Addicts Anonymous meeting.

Woolley stands up and strikes an embarrassed pose. 'My name is Henry and I'm a spendthrift. It's been six weeks since I bought my last roll of toilet paper'.

Leo laughs and slaps the table. 'So we gotta have a Christmas Party this year, Woolley! We'll have it at your place'. Leo gets up and disappears into the bathroom.

'I'll chip in and bring a case of beer!'

Woolley turns to me and lowers his voice. 'Leo says this every year. "I'll bring a case of beer!" But I'm the one who has to buy the food, and I also have to host it'.

Five Days Until Christmas

It's so hot today that waves of heat wobble through Woolley's court-yard. I open the freezer and briefly stick my head inside to cool off. Since my last visit, the health inspector has been and gone, yet still nothing has been done to remove the life-threatening mould.

'Usually it takes up to fourteen working days for them to fix a problem', explains Woolley. 'But with Christmas coming on, it won't be done until next year. I don't blame Public Housing. They're doing the best they can'.

Trailing cigarette smoke, he leads me through the gap in his paling fence and onto a narrow strip of common property. We spot a heavily tanned man sitting in his undies in the sun, drinking yellow liquid from a plastic 1-litre bottle of Coke.

'That's Butch', whispers Woolley. We nod a greeting and continue walking.

'What's in the Coke bottle?' I ask, curious.

'Golden Oak', replies Woolley. 'Butch used to be a two-cask-a-day man. And he lived under the Harbour Bridge. But after he got a home here, he got a job as a cleaner, which he's managed to hang on to for years'.

He points out a honeysuckle tree further ahead. 'Butch is also the building's spotter'.

'What does he look for? The cops?'

Woolley shakes his head. 'The rats'.

At first, I think he is joking. But Woolley tells me that the rats come from three sources: the first is the nearby bay where naval ships dock; the second and third are an old hotel and a community centre on the next block, both of which have been recently renovated and re-plumbed.

'They come up through the pipes', he explains. 'Don nailed chicken wire over our bathroom windows …' – he points up to a mangled screen – '… but the rats ate right through them. For a while there, I thought someone was coming into my unit and stealing my soap all the time. That is, until I saw a cake of Sunlight on the floor of the shower recess, covered in bite marks! Apparently, they like the taste of the fat in the soap'.

We walk up the concrete stairs to the open corridor of the first floor, where the branches of macadamia and umbrella trees form leafy canopies. Woolley knocks on a door and we're soon greeted by Flora, a smiling, petite, Peruvian woman in her late sixties.

He begins to discuss Christmas plans with her: if he organised a party on the day, would she care to come along? Flora is more than enthusiastic. 'He good man!' she announces. 'He very good man! He look after me!'

Woolley promises Flora he will be in touch with the details. I can sense that he still doesn't feel motivated to throw a Christmas party, but it's lonely residents like Flora and Butch who will probably change his mind.

'Flora likes to sew', remarks Woolley, as we walk up the stairs to the second floor. 'She does all my mending for me'.

'Does she charge you for it?'

He glances at me as if I've just asked a silly question. 'When she moved in, we found out she liked to sew. So we sourced a sewing machine for her and hooked her up with the local community centre to take lessons'.

We reach the second landing and are now facing the tops of the many trees. 'There was a neighbour here a couple of years ago, Neil; he had a tumour on his side the size of a basketball'. Woolley pauses and relights his rollie. 'And he couldn't leave his flat because nothing would fit him'.

We continue walking down the corridor. 'So, we went down to Lowes and bought two oversized shirts. Flora cut them up and sewed them into one big shirt. That's how Neil was able to go out when he had cancer'.

Woolley stops in front of a screen door, opens it, and sticks his head in. 'Is it okay to come in?'

'Course it is!' we hear a voice call.

We walk into the unit filled with shelves of books by bestselling author Wilbur Smith. Don's kitchen is equally packed with pots, pans, colanders, utensils and crockery. Don is sitting on a chair in his singlet and shorts, watching the cricket.

'Is it okay if I have a drink?' says Woolley, heading towards the fridge.

'Course you can!' he replies. 'You don't have to ask'.

Woolley returns with a tumbler of Golden Oak and ice and sits across from us. He and Don begin again to discuss the problem with the resident junkie, and how they'll manage him, and the rat and mould problem, over Christmas. They've resorted to buying their own baits and laying them throughout the building.

'Public Housing will not respond in a timely manner', says Woolley in a deliberately mocking tone. 'It's no use putting a Band-Aid on when the body has already bled out'. He lets out a loud huff and reaches for his tobacco. 'It hurts poor people who have been promised help and don't receive it. It hurts'.

Don mentions that Junkie John keeps leaving the laundry door unlocked, which could result in the theft of the building's washers and dryers. More worryingly, John has also been spotted trying to enter the units of his neighbours early in the mornings, while they're still asleep.

'Just one person can fuck it up for everyone else', says Don, wagging his head.

Four Days Until Christmas

Last night, for the first time in sixteen years, Don locked his front door, afraid of Junkie John and his rumoured light fingers. Over his first coffee of the day, Woolley smokes and broods for a while, and soon decides on a plan of action to deal with John over the holidays.

It's mid-morning and already the heat inside his unit is stifling. Sitting at the table, he lights a rollie and rings an officer at Public Housing. After greeting her with the usual niceties, they discuss the problems of the building. Together, they collaborate on a letter for her to type up, photocopy, and send to him, so that he can forward them by hand to all of his neighbours. By composing the letter, rather than making a general complaint, the matter will be dealt with immediately, rather than lingering on into the following year. 'Dear Residents', begins Woolley, 'Just a reminder … that the laundry door is to be kept closed'.

He goes on to cite the reasons why: safety in the event of a fire. He also reminds residents that they must do their washing between the appointed times of 6am and 11pm.

As Woolley continues to talk, Leo appears in the open door, grinning. 'Does this mean we're gunna have a Christmas party?'

Woolley waves to him to be quiet. He clears his throat: 'Finally, it is important that residents … dispose of any unwanted household items … safely'. He draws on his rollie and shifts in his seat. 'Under no circumstances is anything to be thrown from the balconies'.

He winds up the phone call and drops his rollie in the ashtray.

'Does this mean we're gunna have a Christmas party?' Leo repeats.

Woolley stands and smooths down his Hawaiian shirt. 'We're going to have to write up a shopping list', he announces. 'And a guest list, too'.

'I'll throw in a case of beer!' announces Leo, thrilled with this development. 'I'll throw in a case of beer!

Three Days Until Christmas

Multiple copies of the letter that Woolley dictated yesterday have arrived at Ponderosa via Express Post. He rips open the envelope and takes them out. I expect him to begin slipping them under the doors of his neighbours immediately, but first he takes a pencil, turns the letters over, and begins numbering them with a tiny scribble in one corner. Once all twenty-three pages are numbered, he walks out into the corridor and begins making his rounds.

An hour later, with a shopping trolley borrowed from Don, Woolley and Leo make the trek up the hill to Coles. They plan to finance the party through the judicious use of vouchers, which they collect year-round from ATMs and supermarkets.

'Another lurk we've got', says Woolley, following Leo onto the escalator, 'is we volunteer for scientific experiments'. He explains

13

that only just recently he and four other Ponderosa dwellers signed up for medical research into liver function. 'All we had to do was fill out a questionnaire, have a blood test and a liver scan', he says.

We step off the escalator and Leo runs towards the meat section like a kid let loose in a toy shop. 'And for that, we each get a \$20 voucher for Coles', continues Woolley. 'It all adds up, you know'.

We arrive back at Ponderosa, laden with bags of kebabs, bread rolls and frankfurts. As Woolley pulls the shopping trolley along the ground-floor corridor, he spots a balled piece of paper lying in the garden. Shaking his head, he pauses, picks it up, and smooths it out. I can see that it has the Housing NSW logo on the upper left-hand side. Woolley turns the piece of paper over and studies the number pencilled in the corner.

'Bloody Sharkey', he says. 'He's taken a notice about not throwing anything over the balcony – and thrown it over the balcony'.

'Who's Sharkey?' I ask.

'Lives on the third floor', says Woolley.

'He was once a cellmate with Ronald Ryan!' announces Leo. 'With Ronald Ryan! He was once a cellmate with Ronald Ryan!' Woolley notices the puzzled look on my face, and leans in to explain. 'Ronald Ryan was the last man to be hanged in Australia'.

Two Days Until Christmas

We walk outside from Woolley's unit to find someone has tipped white powder all over the trees, the plants, the flowers and the outdoor furniture. Woolley drops to one knee and fingers the coarse, pale granules, lifting a sample to his nose and sniffing expertly, like a forensic scientist analysing a drug sample.

'You reckon it was Sharkey again?' I ask.

'There's only one person in the building who uses this brand of washing powder'. He tilts his head back and gazes up at the third floor.

'Not the junkie again', I say.

Woolley rests his hands on his hips. 'Maybe he thought it was artificial snow'.

Christmas Day

Today, Ponderosa wakes up to more items that have been tossed over the balcony throughout the night: a tube of toothpaste, biscuit wrappers, and what looks like a large puddle of porridge lying on the walkway. 'But it could be spew', observes Woolley, leaning closer.

'One day, that cunt threw a drawer over the balcony', says Don, 'and it crushed a lime tree that I'd just planted'. The avid gardener and chef has been up half the night, marinating and preparing kebabs for the Ponderosa Christmas Party, and he is not impressed by his neighbour's attempts to sabotage the celebration.

Meanwhile, I return to Woolley's unit and inspect the tiny courtyard. Overnight the rats, too, have been hard at work. Three holes the size of basketballs have appeared in the ground, with burrows that curve beneath the paling fence. I glimpse Butch the spotter a few yards down, sitting in the sun, his eyes closed.

While Leo fills recycling bins with bags of ice and beer, Woolley prepares salads and nibblies. A table already sits in the rainforest garden outside, surrounded by empty chairs. At around 4pm, the first of the guests begin to arrive, cradling beers in stubby holders. Leo introduces me to 87-year-old Theo, a pensioner whose unit is rumoured to be the worst affected by the building's mould. As Theo leads me to his door, I notice how impeccably he is dressed on this hot and steamy day: crisp white shirt, a tie, a waistcoat and matching trousers.

When he opens the door, the spore stench hits me before I even cross the threshold. I follow him inside and am shocked to see a thick grey sludge growing across the walls, ceilings and kitchen floor, like some gigantic, toxic blob from the set of a horror film.

Almost gagging, I ask, 'How long has it been like this?'

'Seven years!' he replies, exasperated. 'Seven times they visit to look at the unit. And seven times they do nothing!'

He points to the ceiling of his bathroom, which is sagging so severely it looks as if it's about to collapse. Theo tells me that it's due to a faulty toilet upstairs that, despite many complaints, has never been fixed. He then calls my attention to the shower recess. Sixteen years ago, a former tenant removed the tiled barrier along one side of the recess and so, for the past decade and a half, every time Theo showers, the water runs straight across the floor and into carpet in the living room.

'I'm eighty-seven years old!' cries Theo, shaking a fist. 'They probably wait until I die before they come to fix the place!'

I take photos of the mould and reassure him that I will try to help in any way I can. I lay a hand on his shoulder and invite him back to the party, but he is too upset to socialise – even on Christmas Day. I leave him standing in his kitchen, arms hanging at his side, bewildered by the conditions in which he is forced to live.

Back outside, someone is strumming a guitar. As I walk along the path, a bar stool comes flying over an upstairs balcony, arcs through the air and crashes onto the paving, barely missing Don. Those who are chatting and drinking pause briefly to look over at the missile and return to their conversations. I pop my head into Woolley's unit and am met by Leo, who has been charged with delivering plates of food to any resident too ill or too shy to join us. I offer to help and follow him down the corridor.

He knocks on Butch's door; the door opens a little and Leo passes the plate to a gnarled hand that quickly disappears before the door is slammed shut. 'Butch is too pissed to come to the party', explains Leo. 'But he told me he wanted something to eat'.

Our next visit is to 89-year-old Albert, who opens his door and receives his Christmas meal with gratitude, thanking Leo repeatedly in a soft, strangled voice, before erupting into a coughing fit. For sixteen years, Leo, Woolley and Don have always ensured that Albert has a good, solid meal on Christmas Day.

We climb the stairs to the third floor and stroll along until we come to Sharkey's unit. Leo bangs on the door and suddenly we see the peephole darken.

'Merry Christmas, Sharkey!' cries Leo. He holds up the plate of food.

We can hear Sharkey snorting for a moment, but the eye remains glued to the other side of the peephole.

'Fuck off, Leo!' he shouts.

Leo picks up the last hotdog, flashes his manic grin, leans in close to the peephole, and takes a huge bite.

'Merry Christmas!' he announces, laughing. 'Merry Christmas, Sharkey!'

Wild Frontier:
The Child Gangs of Tweed Heads

(2010)

Dawn has just broken over the rivers of Tweed Heads as volunteer marine rescue worker Martin Grove, sixty-two, cycles home after another eight-hour night shift. Seagulls arc and whirl above him and fishing trawlers cut through curtains of mist. As he turns into his driveway, he suddenly squeezes the brakes and stops short: his car and front yard are strewn with rotting prawn shells, smashed eggs, newspapers, empty bottles and used sanitary pads. This is not the first time he's arrived home to see his property trashed. For the past year a gang of local youths has relentlessly taunted and threatened him – pummelling him with rocks and eggs, cutting off his power cables and accusing him publicly of paedophilia. Martin's many calls to local police so far have proved fruitless – they either don't turn up to take a statement or don't take his complaints seriously.

Martin climbs off his bike and walks through the piles of rubbish towards the verandah. It's then that he sniffs a deeper, ruder stench: his front door and its handle are smeared with shit. He lets himself into the house, grabs his shotgun and loads it.

Gun in hand, he strides up his street, around the block and past a lagoon dotted with small yachts and boats. He knows exactly where the culprits live – it's only a short walk, about two minutes. When he arrives at a white-cladding house on Riviera Avenue, he bangs on the door. A tiny, emaciated woman in her late forties, no taller than a ten-year-old, appears behind the flyscreen, her eyes wide and frightened.

'Where are they?' demands Martin, shaking his gun.

She begins to tremble. 'They're not here', she says, shutting the door.

Martin turns and steps off the verandah, exasperated. He served his country in Vietnam, worked as a miner for a decade, and spent years as his dying mother's only carer, yet nothing has tormented him as much as these local youths. He walks to the centre of the front yard, raises the gun to his head and pulls the trigger; the bullet is launched into the trees, causing the myna birds to shriek and scatter. Unperturbed, Martin knows he has one bullet left. He points the gun to his temple and squeezes the trigger hard.

From across the street the explosion sounds like a car backfiring. A neighbour opens her front door to see a man lying face-up on a lawn, as if he were sunbaking, surrounded by a confetti of blood.

***

I'm standing outside the now-empty suburban house of Martin Grove, who died in hospital twenty-four hours after he shot himself last month. It's a 1970s white brick home with tinted windows the colour of beer, and possibly the most run-down dwelling in the street. A bullet, shot from a .22-calibre rifle some time in 2009, has shattered part of one window. Taped next to it is a sign, 'NSW Police Crime Scene – Under Surveillance', placed there by enraged neighbours after the police refused to declare the property a crime scene. To date no legal action has been taken against any gang member linked with the harassment of and/or violent behaviour towards Grove and his many neighbours. Instead, the youths were offered counselling.

The area that is home to most of these gang members is neither a Public Housing ghetto nor an inner-city slum. On a sunny Monday morning in Tweed Heads West, currawongs chorus and an elderly woman is paddling in an inlet, teaching her dog to swim. Backyards stretch down onto rivers and sandy beaches, and tethered kayaks bob against the tide. The only evidence of any gang activity is a nearby bus stop, graffitied with tags and pornographic images.

This ostensibly quiet suburb, a ten-minute drive from downtown, was developed in the 1970s and '80s and now houses a hybrid community: a combination of private homeowners – mostly retirees, whose properties can fetch up to half a million dollars – and long-term welfare recipients, many of whom are unemployed and living in Public Housing. It's an uneasy alliance.

Having spent my teenage years living in a Melbourne Public Housing estate, I'm acutely aware of how boredom, poverty and society's indifference can unite into a destructive force for working-class and welfare kids, something that's further exacerbated by a disillusioned peer group. In my adolescence, boys sniffed petrol, smashed the windows of parked cars and burned the neighbours' washing hanging on the communal line; girls tattooed themselves using the spike of a broken bottle and a pot of blue ink, got pregnant young then followed their single mothers into a pattern of fortnightly pension cheques and lifelong Public Housing. It was depressing – to be sure – but it wasn't dangerous; there were no violent attacks on innocent neighbours, no persecution of the elderly.

***

Tweed Heads is a border town. Its population of about 56 000 is divided in half, with parts of the south and west side, Tweed Heads, under NSW jurisdiction, while the north-east side, Coolangatta, falls under Queensland law (and is in a different time zone).

The child gangs of Tweed Heads first caught my attention in November 2007, when I read about an eleven-year-old boy who was part of a group that brutally battered an off-duty policeman, Rawson Armitage, and his girlfriend. The couple was walking along an east Coolangatta street late on a Friday night when they were surrounded by at least twenty children and youths, including a teenage girl, who then attacked them. One teenager smashed the unarmed policeman's head so hard against a fence that its very foundations were almost uprooted. His head was then stomped on and his wallet stolen.

Since that attack Tweed Heads has experienced a wave of crime committed by children and youths. According to Martin Grove's brother, Peter, the local gang had harassed Martin to such an extent that, at the time of his suicide, he was preparing to sell his home and move.

In early January 2010, the same youths who'd harassed Martin Grove intimidated and bashed another local resident, Philip Gadsby, a 46-year-old father of two, who lived a block away from the site of Grove's suicide. Phil was riding his bicycle home in broad daylight when the gang of about twenty children and teenagers taunted him with accusations of being a paedophile, pushed him off his bike and hit him over the head repeatedly with a cricket bat. Later in the same week they turned up at his house, with his terrified children and ex-wife Robin inside, and tried to kick his door down. With an injured mouth, distorted by the bashing and the subsequent six stitches he received, Phil was unable to speak, let alone negotiate with the gang members. As the family waited for the police to arrive, Robin finally ran them off, threatening to report and identify them.

I meet Phil in the beer garden of the only pub left in Tweed Heads, the Dolphin. Nicknamed the 'Snake Pit', the 'garden' is a fenced-off area by the car park with a fibreglass roof and two long wooden tables, mostly filled with local men wearing shorts and thongs and holding glasses corseted in stubbie-coolers. Cradling a beer, Phil rises and shakes my hand. He's a tanned, wiry man with his top two front teeth missing. His hands tremble slightly as he re-lights his rollie, still obviously affected by the bashings and threats. 'These kids are absolutely fearless', he says. 'I don't know what they're gonna do next'.

He explains that in the past month he's been harassed or assaulted on five occasions by the same gang. 'I know who they are and I know where they live. I've reported it to the coppers, but no one's been charged'. In fact, a week after the incident with the cricket bat, he called in to the police station to check on the progress of the case and discovered that 'the complaint hadn't even been logged on the computer! There was no record of the bashing'. The police brushed him off with the following statement: 'We'll charge them when Robin makes a statement and identifies the culprits.'

Since the attack Robin has requested repeatedly for the police to do just that – to take her statement and allow her to identify the offenders – but, says Phil, the police don't seem interested in pursuing the matter. Whether the Tweed Heads police are scared, understaffed or just plain indifferent is hard to say, but judging by the atmosphere in the Snake Pit on this Saturday afternoon, the local residents are at their wits' end.

Linda, an ex-nurse whose son developed schizophrenia due to cannabis abuse during his teenage years, drags on her cigarette and leans across the table. 'I've seen groups of kids ambush a cop car and pelt it with beer bottles. And the cops just drive off! They're too scared. This has been going on for years'.

Currently, there are about seven recognised youth gangs in the Tweed area – the Palmy Army, South Side Soldiers, D-Lux, BHQ, Keebra Krew, Dark Neo Soldiers and Coomicub – all of whom, it seems, take great pleasure in terrorising locals. Coomicub, in particular, is responsible for a string of attacks in and around the southern Gold Coast area for the past three years. Naming themselves after a local rap band, its members have 'C' tattoos emblazoned on their bodies. Local police suspect that many members of the Coomicub gang eventually grow up to join the Lone Wolf bikies, who allegedly recently cut off a man's earlobes, then the rest of one ear, in the Currumbin Valley.

In November 2009, a fifteen-year-old boy was arrested for being part of a gang that caused more than $5000 worth of damage to the Tweed Heads indoor pool. Earlier, in August, about a dozen teenagers, armed with knives and metal poles, abducted a sixteen-year-old boy from his Tweed Heads South home, bashed him in remote bushland and left him for dead. (Fortunately he ended up in hospital and recovered.) That same month Murwillumbah High School was broken into and all of the eighteen chickens and roosters that were part of an agricultural program were slaughtered. And, in the space of three months, Kingscliff High School was the site of thirteen break-ins and thefts.

In July 2010, elderly resident Roberta Cross heard a series of explosions: all of her windows had been shattered by shots from air rifles wielded by teenagers who then ran off, laughing. Another woman, in her mid-sixties and who lives alone, was left fearing for her life last year when a group of kids tied a piece of string close to the ground between two posts at the front of her driveway. She tripped over it and fell face-first onto the concrete, badly damaging her face and arms. Like many residents fearful of violent reprisals, she refrained from contacting the police.

Yet another local had faeces smeared on her car, her letterbox blown up, windows smashed, her car graffitied, her fence kicked down and eggs thrown at her house.

It would seem the local police force is overwhelmed, over-worked and perhaps simply over the multiple dysfunctions of Tweed Heads.

***

Here in the Snake Pit it's so hot a woman standing in the doorway pours the dregs of her Bundy and Coke down her cleavage to cool herself. The bearded father of two teenage sons, Booney, who is sitting opposite me, has just been denied another beer for the second time by the barmaid. He glumly sips iced water while Phil and I continue to chat.

Three single mothers, overhearing us, join our table and conversation; two of the three are already drunk. The woman called Wanda, an ex-heroin addict and methadone user, complains that her teenage son's best friend has been missing for four days. She says her son refuses to tell her where his friend is staying, adding that the only way she can get her son, who suffers from Asperger's syndrome, to go to school every day is to stop at McDonald's for breakfast along the way. 'But then', sighs Wanda, swigging on a Bacardi Breezer, 'he just stays for one period then changes out of his school uniform and pisses off for the day'.

Sitting next to her is Fiona, a blue-eyed Aboriginal woman in her late thirties. She admits her teenage son, who suffers from ADHD, runs around with a gang of boys she suspects has been involved in a series of burglaries. 'When he comes home in the morning he could be riding a new bicycle or carrying a new plasma screen. If I ask him where he got them he just says he found them or that someone gave 'em to him'. Fiona shrugs, as if the situation is beyond her control and confesses that she herself was a child gang member during the '80s, after escalating problems with her own mother drove her onto the streets. 'I loved it!' she enthuses. 'I had fun'. But she's quick to add that the gangs of the '80s weren't interested in violence, intimidation or theft. 'We just used to get pissed and do speed and sleep on the beach at night'. Until recently, Fiona's eldest daughter, Kirstie, 19, was part of local gang the South Side Soldiers, the female members of which are referred to as the South Side Sluts.

The man sitting next to Booney, Tom, a dark-skinned giant who reminds me of Chief Bromden in *One Flew Over the Cuckoo's*

Nest, leans across the table and begins telling me about his challenges in raising a teenage boy. His wife was an alcoholic who gave birth to a son with foetal alcohol syndrome and abandoned the baby several days later. Since then, he has raised Locky alone. (His only daughter died of a brain tumour when she was eleven.)

Tom, concerned about the dangers of city life, relocated from Sydney to Tweed Heads to seek a better, slower environment for his 'special needs kid', who is now fifteen. Once Locky began attending the local high school, however, the plan backfired. He began associating with a gang who convinced him to stop taking his medication (lest he become 'a junkie'). Disoriented, Locky would disappear for days at a time with his new friends; when he did return home, Tom would find him asleep on his bed and see the words 'Tweed Breed' inked on his arm. Often in the corner of the room there would be a new television or an iPod still in its original packaging.

'Whaddya gonna do?' moans Booney. 'Lock 'em up?' He gives up trying to roll a joint he's been working on for some time and pockets his bundle of pot. Tom explains that yes, in a way, that is exactly what he has done with his son. Several months ago, he took the radical step of removing Locky from school – and Tweed Heads. He now lives permanently with professional carers on a rural property outside the NSW town of Casino, where he's learning to be a farmer.

The publican taps Booney on the shoulder and announces, 'Ya old lady's looking for ya. Ya better go home'. Booney rolls his eyes and groans. The publican laughs and begins picking up empty glasses. 'It's better to beg for forgiveness', he says, 'than ask for permission'.

I realise the publican's advice could well be the official saying of this unruly place, a border town that has been planned so badly the local council should prostrate itself before the local ratepayers. Until the late '60s, downtown Tweed was flanked by a wide river, with a popular wooden pier, and adjacent parklands. According to Manny, a man in his fifties who has lived here all his life, it was around this time that the council reclaimed the public land and riverbank, filled it in and sold it on. The charming weatherboards and fibro fishing shacks from an earlier era are almost extinct, having been replaced by generic orange brick houses from the '70s and '80s. Now, instead of waterside parks lining one side of the main street, it is dominated by chainstores such as Liquorland, Coles, Woolworths, McDonald's, Hungry Jack's, and their sprawling car parks.

'Fifty years ago there were three times as many people around on the streets', says Manny. 'Today, it's a fucking ghost town'. Indeed, this is a city built around the motor vehicle rather than the pedestrian. Scores of car dealerships line the main street yet there are only two restaurants.

'The council doesn't like young people around here', adds Mark, also a lifelong local, gesturing at the cluster of cars outside the local bowling club. Inside, pensioners shuffle around playing pokies, Keno results are announced over a PA, and a man on crutches sells raffle tickets for a meat tray.

It comes as no surprise when I learn that the Tweed Shire has the second-highest population of over-65s in NSW, just behind the retirement haven of beachside Port Macquarie. And, as I walk around, it's obvious that the council has prioritised the needs and predilections of the retirees and tourists moving here from other regions over the local families and children. It feels like a place where people come to die.

To make matters worse, most of the youth gang members live in the southern and western suburbs of Tweed, 8 kilometres from the city centre, yet most public transport stops at 6pm. The only recreational amenity in the area for children and teenagers is a concrete skate park that was built recently next to the local high school. It has since become a common meeting place for the gangs at night.

'When I grew up here it was beautiful, a little village', recalls Manny, who lives with his elderly mother and his brother. 'When we were their age we went surfing, hunting and fishing. [But] this is a new generation of shit'. Two years ago Manny was attacked by a group of six kids aged around fourteen and fifteen. He had to rip a branch off a tree to defend himself and scare them off. Now he doesn't go out at night and, like most locals, keeps a cricket bat inside his front door. Along the route he takes from the pub to his home, he's even hidden weapons in particular places as a precaution.

'They sit on their arses all day, watching TV and playing computer games', he continues. 'Then at sunset, they start texting one another and meeting up to cause trouble. Now they're doing this shit in daylight. Why should anyone have to lock themselves in their own house?'

***

According to local MP Geoff Provest, the area is beset with intense drug and alcohol abuse. 'The Tweed Shire has the third-highest percentage of arrests for the production and/or distribution of illegal substances in the state, behind only Cabramatta and Kings Cross. It's the major manufacturing port supplying drugs for south-western Queensland'. Provest explains that 53 kilograms of illicit drugs were confiscated in the Tweed–Byron Local Area Command in 2009, including over 3500 cannabis plants, 'yet the Tweed–Byron Local Area Command does not even have a dedicated drug squad. And, on top of all that, the Tweed Shire also has the highest incidence of drink driving per capita in the country'.

Provest adds that Tweed Heads is the fastest growing regional area in the state – it's actually becoming an outer suburb of Brisbane – yet there's very little reliable public transport. All juvenile parole officers are based in Lismore and it takes an hour by bus to get there. Also, the new P-plate laws have caused problems. Novice drivers are only allowed one passenger after 11pm. 'Usually, these kids would be getting a lift home', he says, 'but now they're back on the streets'.

During 2010, in the Tweed Shire, there were 2200 reports of child neglect and/or abuse, with about eighty kids removed from their homes by DOCS. 'The parents know that if their kids are going to be removed they'll lose most of their welfare benefits', says Provest. 'So what they do is move the family over the border into Queensland for six months – look, it could be only a few blocks away from their residence in NSW – but because it's a different state, their files don't follow them and they start all over again with Queensland welfare'. And apparently, if Queensland's Department of Communities does begin a separate investigation, the same family simply disappears over the border, back into NSW.

Provest tells me he often goes out on police patrols at night so he stays in touch with the multiple problems facing the community. The police, he says, 'often pick up kids as young as ten and eleven wandering around the streets in the early hours of the morning with nowhere to go. When the police drop them off at their houses, most of the time, the parents aren't even home'. He adds: 'These gangs are committing some terrible crimes, but at least a gang will care about these kids and look after them'.

It's clear to me that the dysfunction in the town extends way beyond uncontrollable kids and an uncomprehending, ageing pop-ulation. It seems as if there's an entire generation that has gone miss-ing – the one that should be between the children and retirees. Most of the mothers and fathers I've met thus far are single parents who live on welfare. All but three of the thirty-odd I have spoken to admit to regularly imbibing alcohol and drugs. Hardly any work full-time and most have no plans to do so. No wonder Provest is currently raising funds for a youth refuge in Tweed Heads; I find myself thinking that, while he's at it, he should consider opening a second refuge for many of the parents.

***

Phil Gadsby has invited me to Riviera Avenue to meet a few other people who have been terrorised by the local kids. Frustrated by the lack of police protection, his neighbours have heard I'm in town and are both anxious to talk to me about their problems and relieved that someone is finally paying attention. All except Phil insist on anonymity; they refuse to be photographed and are too scared to walk down the street with me, past the houses where the gang members live. Even the local journalist who has reported on child gang activities in the *Tweed Daily News* for the past two years confesses that he publishes those articles without a by-line because his kids go to the same school as the gang members and he fears for their safety.

Phil's neighbour – we'll call him Steve – tells his story rapidly, as if he's being timed and is trying to beat the clock. A few weeks ago, Steve's six-year-old son was riding his scooter out the front of their house and made a passing remark to one of the gang members, who took offence and began swearing at and threatening the boy. Steve confronted the teenager and tried to get rid of him and his mates. When they wouldn't move on, Steve kicked the troublemaker in the knee, which resulted in him being attacked by six gang members in his front yard. Steve rang the police to report the incident; they turned up to take his statement two hours later.

In an echo of Phil's dealings with the police, when Steve went to check on the progress of the complaint there was no record of it. 'They hadn't even logged it in the computer ... They only took down notes at my place and that was the end of it'. Steve sighs heavily and shrugs his shoulders. 'Almost everyone around here has been attacked. They've all had their houses pummelled with rocks, windows smashed. These kids just think the cops and the law are a joke'.

Between them, in the past two months, Phil and Steve have contacted the police more than eight times over separate incidents of gang harassment and violence, with little attention or co-operation in return. Off the record, one policeman advised Steve to defend himself, a suggestion he has taken seriously. 'Now I keep an axe, a cricket bat and a fishing rod beside the front door'.

The son of a Mormon bishop, Steve now sits up all night, every night, waiting for the next attack, only allowing himself to fall asleep when the sun comes up. Like Phil, he has a contingency plan for his kids if the gang strikes again: they will either hop over the back fence and run to a neighbour's house, or run to the bathroom and lock the door. Steve has installed a removable doorknob on the same door for further protection. 'I've had about a dozen people willing to back me up', adds Phil, glancing at his damaged front door. 'I've got a list of names. I've even had people offer me guns'.

Phil tells me that after he reported his fourth assault to the police, he made an off-the-cuff remark to the attending officer: 'We should get together our own gang and deal with this ourselves. Bash the shit out of them'.

The officer allegedly replied, 'That wouldn't be a bad idea'.

Incredulous, Phil asked if he was joking.

The policeman shook his head. 'No, we can't do anything till we catch them in the act. But if you can deal with it yourselves we'll turn a blind eye'.

Steve folds his arms and nods. 'I've already warned the cops that I'll be looking after myself now. I said, "Next time, I won't be calling you. I'll be calling an ambulance – not for me, but for them"'.

He pauses, folding his leg to rest one foot on his other knee. 'I know I could go to jail', he confesses, 'but I've got to protect my family'.

***

The rate of absenteeism in the Tweed–Byron police force is unusually high. In 2009, Tweed Heads NSW Police Association representative Troy Hamilton admitted about 26 per cent of their officers were unavailable for full-time work. 'The command as at the end of November 2009 had thirteen officers on long-term sick leave, thirteen officers on restricted duties and sixteen officers classified as part-time', Mr Hamilton said. Even the area's head-of-command, Tweed–Byron Superintendent Michael Kenny, went on sudden and indefinite sick leave on 30 December 2009. Three months later he is yet to return.

A number of the police stations in the area are staffed only during office hours rather than twenty-four hours a day, a situation that led to the near-fatal bashing of the Indian student Sachin Surendran in June 2009, on the steps of the Coolangatta Police Station, which is only open between 8am and 5pm. 'There is no point in having a police station if it's not always open', Surendran said in late 2009, before fleeing the country and returning to India permanently.

In September 2009, Tweed Heads police, overwhelmed by juvenile crime, took the extraordinary step of urging parents to dob in their kids to the law. But of course it's difficult for parents to report their children if they don't know where they are, or, even worse, don't care. Last October, the NSW government approved legislation to fine parents up to $2500 for a first offence of failing to ensure their children attend school. But, as Clarence Nationals MP Steven Cansdell notes, 'Magistrates can fine parents all they want but they are not going to pay the fine because they have not got the money to start with'.

Curious to speak with the local constabulary, I ring Tweed Heads area crime manager Sergeant Greg Carey, requesting an interview. 'Have you spoken to the police media yet?' he demands. When I answer no, he tells me that I have to request permission from a liaison office in Sydney first. I remind him that in the past few months he's been quoted frequently in the local newspaper. 'That's local media', he replies. 'Not national'.

'So you're telling me that I'm not allowed to speak to any police officer in Tweed Heads while I'm here?'

'No', he replies firmly. 'Not without permission'.

He gives me a Sydney number to call and when I do the answering officer gives me an email address, telling me to send through an outline of my subject matter and a request to interview Sergeant Carey. I do this immediately and also include my full contact details and the direct number of Sergeant Carey.

One, two, then three days pass and I still haven't received a reply from the Sydney liaison officer, the media supervisor, or indeed any representative of the Tweed Heads police. I can't seem to shake a niggling suspicion that they are collectively indifferent, or have something to hide, or both.

***

'The cops aren't interested in catching these kids', says Les, the owner of a burger bar on Kennedy Drive in Tweed Heads West. The police, he adds, 'just sit on their arses all day in their cars down at the intersection, either fining people for making an illegal right-hand turn or breathalysing them'.

On his mobile phone he shows me photos of two male friends: their eyes are black and swollen shut, their lips are split and their faces are ravaged with cuts and bruises, as if they're victims of a serious car accident. Six months ago, explains Les, they were walking home after a night shift at the resort Twin Towns when they were attacked by a group of youths who beat them badly, 'just for something to do'. Even though the men can identify the kids, this particular gang still remains at large.

'It's like a teenager trying to get out of the washing-up every night', complains Phil Gadsby's twin sister, Kerry, referring to the inaction of the local police. We're sitting outside the burger bar, sipping coffee. Like her brother, Kerry is short and wiry, and as she speaks her hands dart around in the air. 'And parents need to stop playing the victim', she adds. 'A lot of single mothers and fathers up here spend their money on drugs, alcohol and gambling – not their kids. I gave up alcohol years ago and I still go to AA. It can be done'.

'Phil's rung me up a couple of times in the past week', says Kerry, gazing down at her upturned hands. 'He's told me he's suicidal. I'm so worried about him. He's ready to jump off a bridge'. She tells me that Phil had already been juggling problems before the bashings began last month: finances, work, and his girlfriend, who desperately needs a kidney transplant. 'He was barely coping as it was, but to be attacked and harassed on top of it …' her voice trails off and she glances at the passing traffic. 'Now his kids are too scared to leave the house'.

Since the most recent attack on Phil, Kerry has rallied the local community to reject vigilante action and instead lobby for tough new curfew laws. 'Any kids out on the street after sunset, their parents should be fined'. It sounds reasonable in theory, but I wonder how effective the proposed curfews will be, considering that the parents themselves are often not at home.

'My concern is for the next generation', Kerry explains. 'I don't want to see any more people get hurt'. A few minutes later, she introduces me to someone from this 'next generation', an Aboriginal teenager who has been friends with local gang members since primary school. Sienna sports bleached blonde hair and nose rings, though she's nervy and tense and slumps in her plastic chair, as if trying to make herself seem smaller. Sienna tells me she has made a list of names of the lead members of the gang that intimidated Martin Grove and attacked Phil Gadsby (and many others in the area), but says the police weren't interested in pursuing the matter.

Sienna insists that once a kid becomes a member of a particular gang it can be difficult, if not impossible, to leave. As a consequence of the 2007 bashing of Rawson Armitage and his girlfriend, one of Sienna's closest friends, gang member Roland, was sent to juvenile detention for three weeks. After his release he tried to reform himself but was soon drawn back into the group through persistent peer pressure. Not long after, the same gang members, including Roland, were arrested for attempted robbery – this time Roland almost went to jail. With the help and encouragement of his girlfriend, Roland again tried to 'go straight' and leave. The other members responded by threatening to kill his grandmother, who is in her late sixties. When Roland refused to return to the gang, they did indeed attack his grandmother, leaving her bruised and battered. The poor woman was too scared of the gang to report the assault to the police or even attend the local hospital. According to Sienna, when the bashing of his grandmother failed to return Roland to the fold, the gang turned up at his door with a gun and threatened to shoot him. 'The girlfriend was the one who changed Roland and got him out. Now he's working full-time. But now the gang wants to kill them both'.

Listening to her stories, delivered with an odd mixture of resignation and bravado, I'm shocked by how hopeless life seems for these kids, even for the ones who attempt to forge a more prosperous future. When I ask her what it's like to grow up here, she squirms in her seat and frowns. 'Tweed's scumville', she says. 'It's full of wankers. Everywhere you walk there's someone trying to bash you'.

She admits that when she was in primary school, she was expelled for throwing a chair at another Indigenous student, who called her 'a wigger' ('white nigger'). It was only in 2008, at the age of seventeen, and after more than 800 reports of bad behaviour on her high school record, that Sienna made a concerted effort to change. 'I realised that if I didn't get my shit together I was gonna end up just like them. I'm just trying not to hang out with wankers.'

In 2009, Sienna completed her Higher School Certificate and went on to study children's services at TAFE. In her final year of school she studied Aboriginal painting and found that she has a talent for it. She's planning to teach painting to local kids, 'for free at first, and then we'll see what happens'.

***

I say goodbye to Sienna, Kerry and Les and hail a taxi to take me down Riviera Avenue. We approach the home of members of the gang that locals believe is responsible for the bashings of Phil Gadsby and others. I see a manicured front lawn lined with saplings, the same lawn on which Martin Grove shot himself dead only a few weeks earlier. Lying on the grass are two bicycles and an upturned skateboard.

The house is single-storeyed and white, with a carport to one side. It all looks so impossibly suburban and innocuous it's hard to imagine the home is also the unofficial headquarters of a violent gang. The taxi pulls up and, as I climb out onto the street, I ask the driver to wait.

I walk onto the shaded, concrete verandah. Peering through the locked screen door, I am quietly amazed to see a perfectly neat living room with a polished coffee table, and rows of figurines; in the background a television murmurs an ad for KFC. For a moment I think I've arrived at the wrong house. I knock on the door and a short thin woman in her late forties appears on the other side of the screen, her face so drawn and haunted she looks more like an apparition than a human being. When I explain why I'm here, her hand flies to her throat and she begins to tremble. I feel a rush of empathy for her – for this frightened twig of a woman whose husband works all night and who is clearly struggling to raise three wild teenage boys.

Voice shaking, she tells me her two older sons are not at home, but she'd be prepared to speak with me 'under the right circumstances'. I ask her what the right circumstances might be. She hesitates before replying. 'Once I get permission from my husband'.

When I hear her say this, my heart sinks, knowing I'll never hear from her again. As she unlocks the screen door to take my card and phone number, her youngest son, aged about twelve, appears by her side and peers at me with curiosity. His eyes are bright; he has a shock of blond hair and his tanned face is beginning to peel, just like thousands of other average Australian kids. The neatness of the house combined with the boy's ordinariness and good health unsettle me further, as if all the information and accounts I've gathered so far might not be true after all.

But my confusion quickly dissipates when I climb back into the cab and we begin to drive down the block. A boy is standing in the middle of the road, his back turned away from me, wearing only a pair of board shorts, his arms and legs stretched out, as if deliberately trying to block our way. He's probably only fifteen or so, but his sun-tanned back is tattooed with a galaxy of blue stars – the Southern Cross – that glint in the sunlight.

The driver slows down and, as the boy moves to one side, I glimpse his wide blue eyes, high cheekbones, the sweat pearling down his neck – a blond-haired Adonis who wouldn't look out of place on a New York catwalk or in an Armani catalogue.

I catch my breath, smile, and lean out the window, trying to draw him into a conversation. 'Hi', I announce. 'How're you going?'

Suddenly his chiselled features retract into a scowl and he spits on the hood of the taxi. 'Piss off, ya stupid bitch', he barks. 'You don't belong around here'.

The Hordes

(2013)

Aunty Avril first exhibited symptoms shortly after her second husband died. Anything that was carried into the house rarely made it back out, no matter how insignificant or useless. As a child visiting her I would marvel at the towers of old newspapers mouldering in her sunroom, like a city skyline, and wondered when she'd find the time to read them all. In the front room a grand piano stood covered in broken picture frames, plastic flowers, headless dolls, and knitting needles. Before she became a hoarder she was a devoted scrimper: she covered all her furniture in plastic and once made my father drive half an hour out of his way to save three cents on a cabbage.

The hallway doubled as her second closet. From the picture rails hung layer upon layer of floral dresses from the 1950s, and walking to the bathroom always afforded a cottony whiff of mildew. In fact, walking anywhere in the house was a challenge, because once plastic garbage bags were invented she began collecting them, too – not to store in a kitchen cupboard for the disposal of rubbish, but to help her curate her vast accumulation of stuff. There were only two armchairs in the living room – one for her, and one for her forty-year-old son, Norman, who'd never left home (no, not even has he made it out of the house for longer than a few hours in his entire life). The armchairs were parked directly in front of a portable TV, which they'd watch together while eating their dinners from fold-out tray tables. The rest of the room was devoted to the bulging garbage bags, walls of them stacked on top of one another, past the windowsill and fireplace, as if in fortification against a dangerous flood. Even as a kid I found my aunt intriguing: everyone on my father's side was a tad unusual but Aunty Avril was in a league of her own. As a teenager, she would always steal her younger sister's boyfriends and add them to her collection.

Avril hoarded all the family photographs dating back to the mid-nineteenth century and refused to share them or even loan the negatives. I only found this out when one day I was visiting and noticed a line of picture frames on the mantelpiece, the glass panes of which were covered in so much dust I couldn't see the figures behind them. I picked one up and rubbed and scraped until an image finally emerged: five tall, dark-haired men with long black beards and insouciant gazes, all the image of the bushranger Ned Kelly. Avril informed me that they were my Irish grandmother's brothers, known colloquially as the Murphy Boys. I stupidly asked her if I could keep the photograph, then asked if I could take it down to the chemist and have it copied, and then I finally gave up and put it back on the shelf.

Avril died in the late 1990s and in her will left her home and all its contents to Norman, and to her daughter, Vonnie, who by then was divorced and had returned to live in the art deco house, moving back in to her childhood bedroom still filled with ringleted dolls, baby shoes and one-eyed teddy bears. The state of Avril's home had been a topic of conversation among the family for years – nearly everyone at one time or another had tried to persuade her to clear it out. But Avril had always stubbornly refused any offer of assistance, not allowing the removal of a single magazine or hairpin.

Naturally, we all assumed that now Avril was gone from the house permanently the results of her fifty years of hoarding would soon follow. Norman and Vonnie would be able to enjoy an uncluttered, healthier house and perhaps begin to invite friends and relatives over. I'd even be able to access the family archival photos and have them copied for myself and for future generations.

I rang them up and suggested that I visit them both, also promising that I'd bring some lunch. 'Don't come tomorrow', said Vonnie, now in her mid-fifties. 'We need some time to clean up'.

When I climbed out of the cab, the house was just as I had remembered it: curved corners, lead glass windows, a portico's crumbling pillars. But the garden was overgrown with weeds, the once blooming rose bushes had long since died, and the fishpond was empty and rutted with deep crevices. My cousins greeted me at the front door and ushered me inside. In spite of the promised clean-up, the furniture and paintings were entombed in dust, the grand piano was covered in detritus, and every room was crammed with even more bulging garbage bags. Avril's collection of newspapers had been extended to the living room, where they sat in columns against the wall.

In the cramped kitchen, there was only enough room for two chairs, and so over lunch we had to take turns sitting at the table. The original Kookaburra enamel stove was still there, built into a fireplace, but instead of cooking on it, my cousins used the oven as a dispensary for their many prescriptions and medicines (both suffered respiratory problems due to lack of ventilation).

After lunch we filed back into the living room so I could look again at the old family photographs – and perhaps now borrow them – when Vonnie mentioned that their TV had broken down and unfortunately they'd been unable to replace it.

'Why haven't you been able to get a new one?' I asked. 'Are they too expensive?'

Norman shook his head and pointed to a 10-centimetre gap between two towers of yellowing newspapers. 'We can't find a TV small enough to fit into that space'.

The Tincture of Health

(2010)

An emaciated man is begging for help on the back verandah of the Nimbin Hemp Embassy, an organisation lobbying for cannabis law reform. His breathing is shallow and he trembles slightly. For the past six years Mike has endured dialysis treatment for kidney disease and was recently diagnosed with terminal cancer. In a faltering voice, he describes how the medications prescribed by his doctors, particularly morphine, produce too many side effects and are making him even more ill: he is in constant pain and can no longer eat properly.

Tony Bower, a bearded Aboriginal man of fifty-five, calmly listens to Mike's complaints, nodding, and gestures for Mike to take a seat. He then disappears inside the Hemp Embassy, an old, rambling wooden building on Nimbin's main street, and returns with two homemade tinctures. As Mike takes the vials he wilts a little, as if he's just been relieved of a massive burden. When Tony explains the required dosages, Mike announces: 'I'm pissing off the morphine. This stuff's so much better'.

For over a decade, Tony has cultivated marijuana for medicinal use on a country property in northern NSW. He delivers it in tincture form to any ill person within two days drive of his home. For those in more remote areas, he sends the bottles by post. He refuses to charge for his medicine, and is not even reimbursed for the cost of production. 'I've explained to the government and the cops that I am Aboriginal and it is against my culture to refuse help or comfort to someone in need'.

We sit together on the balcony of the Hemp Embassy, which overlooks a lush valley. Tony explains that, in the early '80s, a near-fatal motorcycle accident left him with scores of broken bones and steel plates in his legs; it took him more than two years to recover. As he talks, he gestures to his calves and their fretwork of deep, pink scars. He tells me that it was during his recuperation, when he suffered unrelenting pain, that he began experimenting with, and growing, a variety of marijuana seeds.

A court appearance for cultivation of cannabis in 1999 effectively left him with permission to grow up to forty-nine plants for personal use. Since then, however, he's discovered a widespread need for his product, which necessitates growing many more plants. The licensing for these is proving difficult and currently he is in a legal no-man's-land.

Tony leads me down the stairs from the verandah and through a paddock behind the embassy, where his white campervan is parked. I glance about, impressed by this unofficial mobile cannabis dispensary, the only one operating in Australia: a double bed at the back, a gas stove, a table set up for consultations and, most importantly, a portable fridge in which to store the tinctures. The entire van is impeccably clean and tidy.

Tony sits back as we chat, and puffs on a wooden pipe. He explains that the medicinal use of cannabis is legal in Canada, Austria, the Netherlands, Spain, Israel, Italy and in fourteen states of the US (with another twelve indicating an intention to legalise the herb). Currently, he says there are more than 1100 government-run dispensaries operating in Los Angeles alone. 'But the stuff they prescribe there is a synthetic cannabinoid called Marinol. All my tinctures are made from organic products and they're a hell of a lot more effective than that synthetic stuff'.

In 2009, the Australian Therapeutic Goods Administration approved the use of a British drug called Sativex, a mouth-spray made from botanical material. To access Sativex, however, doctors must apply for a special authority from the federal Department of Health and negotiate a bureaucratic labyrinth. 'Meanwhile, people are suffering and dying in pain, and I have a product that works', Tony says.

A father of three and grandfather of eight, Tony survives on a disability pension. In addition to growing and harvesting his private crop of medical marijuana, he also distils his own pure-grain alcohol to use as a base for the tincture medication. For his oil-based medicines, he uses hemp oil.

He tells me that the tincture usually begins taking effect within five minutes of administration. 'There was this one bloke I treated', says Tony, grinning, 'who'd just had a back operation and couldn't even stand up. Fifteen minutes after taking the tincture he was not only out of bed, he was walking around'. Tony is quick to add, however, that his tinctures don't work for everyone and some still need to take synthetic painkillers. 'But if I can get a patient early on in their treatment, I find they have little need for high doses of other drugs, especially morphine'.

I wonder aloud about the potential abuse of his product by people not genuinely suffering from an illness. He smiles and nods again. 'You can't get stoned on my tinctures, which is why the older ones like it so much'. He adds that many of the pensioners he's treated don't like the idea of smoking marijuana, and that those who have eaten marijuana-laced cookies find themselves laughing too much and feeling out of control. 'All my product does is provide pain relief, increase appetite and energy, and ensure a good night's sleep – without any side effects'.

He tells another story of a woman in her eighties who, suffering from cancer, had been bedridden for two years. 'Within days of her first tincture treatment, she was out in the backyard, gardening.

Her son couldn't believe it'. He then relates a story about two terminally ill men he met recently, men whose emphysema was so bad they couldn't even walk down the driveway for a consultation with Tony. 'After a week of treatment', says Tony, 'their lung capacity was tested and it was three times greater'. The reason for this, he explains, is that marijuana is a powerful anti-inflammatory, particularly for the lungs, and is possibly ten times stronger than aspirin.

'The only problem with those two blokes', concedes Tony, 'is that they're feeling so good now, they think they've been cured and have taken up smoking again'. Tony shakes his head and shrugs. He believes that once most people start taking his tinctures regularly, they find they can reduce or even stop taking certain synthetic medications altogether. He suspects that this is why the government won't respond to repeated requests for clinical trials of his tinctures: they have too much invested in the pharmaceutical companies.

Tony has spent years writing to both federal and state governments, sharing his research, sending samples and urging them to set up official trials so his product can be independently tested. 'Every time we get a new premier I get the same letter, but with a different signature on the bottom'.

In 2008, a letter from the office of the federal minister for health and ageing, Nicola Roxon, acknowledged Tony's compassionate actions, but also informed him that it is illegal to produce cannabis products for anything but approved scientific and medicinal purposes, adding that 'no pharmaceutical form of medicinal marijuana could be approved unless an application is made to the Therapeutic Goods Administration with supporting data from clinical trials, which enables an assessment of its quality, safety and efficacy'.

In response to the letter, Tony compiled a 129-page submission of his research and forwarded it with samples of his product to the TGA – along with the application fee of $1600. Within a week, the cheque was cashed, but over a year has passed and a decision is yet to be made about his application.

He explains that there are between 150 and 200 strains of marijuana in Australia, and it has taken him years of trial and error to develop the one that produces the most efficacious tincture. 'I've actually developed my own variety', he says. 'I've been wanting to register it with the Therapeutic Goods Administration, but they refuse to co-operate with me'. He shakes his head. 'The irony is, in Australia we have the best climate in the world for the cultivation of marijuana, yet we're doing nothing with it'.

Of course, by this stage, I'm keen to try some of the tincture myself. Lately, I've been suffering from insomnia and a recent sprain in my right foot has left me limping. I don't have a letter from my doctor verifying my condition, though, and I certainly don't want to jeopardise Tony's crusade.

Later that night I'm having a beer with one of Tony's patients who is being treated for a range of problems: pancreatitis, arthritis, depression. She places an amber bottle in front of me and urges me to sample a capful of the oily liquid. I hesitate – albeit briefly – then obediently down the medicine.

Maybe it is the beer or Nimbin's fresh air, but that night I sleep right through until midday the next day. And later, when I join my nephews – aged eight and ten – busking on the main street, I dance to their music for an hour without a twinge of pain.

Flying High:
The Rise and Guise of
Self-Funded Retirees

(2014)

In the late 1990s, my 78-year-old father used to fly to the northern NSW town of Lismore several times a year, buy $10 000 worth of marijuana, store it in his carry-on luggage, and fly back to Sydney the same day. As a lifelong user of cannabis, in his old age he began dealing it as well in order to supplement both his habit and his paltry old-age pension. At the time, I considered him an entrepreneurial anomaly, but these days more and more Australian pensioners are cultivating and/or selling illegal drugs – and for a myriad of reasons. Anecdotal evidence suggests that some do it for the promise of regular visitors, others to fund hobbies, yet others to be able to afford to self-medicate with illegal drugs. Most, however, seem to be happy to be on the wrong side of the law for the chance to top up their pension cheques with tax-free cash.

Brian Ogilvie, for example, was a lonely 68-year-old pensioner who lived in a caravan in Mackay, Queensland, when he decided to become a drug dealer in 2008. His wife had died forty years previously and he'd been on anti-depressants for three decades. A former fisherman and council worker, he'd grown bored and isolated being on his own and so opened his caravan for business. He treated his dozen or so customers as friends, serving tea and sandwiches for them whenever they came over to score, before he was raided and charged in 2010.

'There's no money. You can't live off the pension', said 71-year-old Alan Hogan, as he stood in the dock of the Maroochydore District Court in December 2012, in yet another example of a retiree struggling financially. 'I can't work. I had a shoulder reconstruction'. Police who searched his Cooroibah property in July 2011 found a sophisticated hydroponic set-up behind a cupboard that could only be opened with a single key. They also discovered 2 kilograms of cannabis, forty plants, and over $1000 in a drawer. Hogan was sentenced to two years in jail, to be suspended after he'd served eight months.

Meanwhile, over in Western Australia, in the same month, an eighty-year-old man was arrested during a raid in Broome after being caught selling cannabis from the front door of his property. In 2012, the court was told Ahma Bin Haji Mohamed Noor lived on a pension of about $400 a week. The magistrate noted that the retiree had a history of similar offences and had been fined $600 only eighteen months before. After being fined again for $2000, Noor was warned that if he were arrested again, he'd be going straight to jail. Later, a 78-year-old woman who lived in a Sydney Public Housing unit was charged with selling cannabis from her home, after a police raid located a large amount of cannabis and cash, scales and other drug paraphernalia. Not long afterwards, a couple of grey nomads in their mid-sixties, from South Australia, were charged with trafficking. Police discovered that a purpose-built compartment had been installed inside the undercarriage of their caravan, which hid sixteen packages, each containing about 450 grams of cannabis. At the time, police alleged the couple was planning to sell the product interstate.

Recent statistics have found that more than a quarter of older Australians struggle financially. The *Global AgeWatch Index 2013* is the first international league table ranking the welfare of people

aged over sixty. The *Index* reported that Australia's overall ranking was diminished by the financial circumstances of older people,
with 27 per cent having an income less than half the country's average – trailing behind Sweden, Norway, Germany, the Netherlands,
Canada, New Zealand, the US and the UK. It's little wonder that
our elders are peddling drugs in order to make ends meet.

***

It's Saturday morning on the main street of Nimbin and the footpath is alive with stalls of handmade clothes, jewellery, jars of jams,
and floppy hats. Buskers play raucous trombones and drums, tod-
dlers run around barefoot, and unleashed dogs wander in and out of
cafés, nosing for scraps of food. Everyone, it seems, wants to sell you
something – from the skinny man flogging clay ocarinas, to what is
locally known as 'the Lane Boys' (young men who hang around the
main street, hawking weed to tourists who arrive on buses several
times a day).

As I walk beneath the awnings, above the din I hear a high-
pitched voice crying, 'Cookies! Cookies!' and look ahead to glimpse
a plump older woman waving a small plastic bag in the air like a
miniature flag. Her face is deeply lined, her grey hair is swept up
into a roll and she's wearing a loose orange and black kaftan and a
pair of rubber thongs. The bag she is holding contains three round
biscuits.

'How much?' I ask.

'Three for twenty, or six for thirty.'

I nod and sit down beside her on a milk crate. When I tell
her I'm writing a story about pensioner drug dealers she agrees to
talk to me under the condition that I don't reveal her real name or
address. A mother of two and grandmother of five, 'Nanna', now in
her late sixties, worked full-time as a nurse in Sydney before retir-
ing to northern NSW. Seven years ago, in order to supplement her

old-age pension, she began baking marijuana cookies and selling them two days a week to day-tripping tourists.

'Why only two days a week?' I ask. 'Is it because you get tired?'

She shakes her head. 'It's not that. The Lane Boys get the shits. They don't like me moving in on their territory'.

A group of young Asian men shuffles past. Nanna jumps to her feet and waves the bag again. 'Cookies!' she trumpets, in a voice so warm and maternal that they stop and enquire about her prices. As she quietly negotiates with the non-English speakers I can see why the Lane Boys feel so threatened by Nanna. Scoring from the Lanes requires handing cash over to a paranoid and pimple-faced stranger, following him down several back lanes, where the cash is handed over to yet another paranoid and pimpled-faced stranger, who disappears beneath a house or onto the roof of a café, and returns with your marijuana in a paper bag. Buying home-baked cookies on the main street from a woman who looks as harmless and gentle as your grandmother is an appealing alternative to the cloak-and-dagger high jinks of the boys. And it obviously works: a few moments later one Asian man is handing over cash and Nanna is whispering to him to hide his purchase in his jacket pocket before the coppers spot them.

As she sits back down I ask her if she's ever been arrested. She brushes a stray grey tendril away from her face and nods. 'I've been raided three times', she admits, 'and busted twice'. The last time, in 2011, she explains, she was fined $365, and let off on a two-year good behaviour bond.

'But that still hasn't stopped you?'

She smiles and shouts, 'Cookies!' again to three passing people so pale and fair I wonder if they could be albinos.

Nanna admits she doesn't grow or harvest the marijuana plants herself, but sources them through a local grower. She tells me she's never been a recreational user of weed ('Oh, I had a toke or two when I was nineteen years old, but didn't everybody?'). Instead, she eats half of one of her own cookies every night – and has done so for the past seven years – for relief from arthritic pain and to help her sleep soundly.

The albinos are now at a nearby ATM and are glancing back at Nanna. I ask her how much she makes in a week, and she replies, 'Depends on the weather and the time of year'. As I watch notes slide out of the ATM slot and snatched by a pale hand, she adds, 'Roughly between 100 and 600 for the weekend'.

The albinos return and the deal is done within several discreet seconds. The cash disappears into Nanna's bra and cookies are sequestered in a buyer's bum bag. As the albinos leave, Nanna warns them in a voice reminiscent of the caring nurse she once was, 'Remember it takes an hour to kick in. And don't drive a car, all right? It's far too dangerous!'

***

In Byron Bay there is a gift shop on the main street, filled with candles, tie-dyed saris, feathered dream catchers and Balinese bells. As you step through the door you'll inhale the scent of incense, and when you walk past the stands of homemade soaps and trinkets, towards the back of the shop, you'll notice a small door, standing ajar. If you nudge it open you'll see a small, enclosed verandah, cluttered with boxes of stock, and a desk littered with papers, and plastic lunch bags filled with marijuana.

You'll probably also glimpse a balding man named Lotus, whose silver hair and beard make him look like a well-tanned Gandalf, perched over the desk and weighing up buds or trimming stalks from dried plants. Though today, when I pop my head around the door, he's sitting on a red towel on the floor, shirtless, and trying to salvage some stock – some sheets of fluorescent smiley-face stickers that were wet during last night's storm. The tin roof is still leaking and the tiny area smells like damp dog fur.

Lotus looks up and gestures to me to take a seat. As he continues to dry and stack the stickers, I ask him how long he's been selling pot from here in the back room of his legitimate retail business.

He pauses and pulls on his beard. 'About ten years', he replies.

Now in his late sixties, Lotus tells me he began smoking weed when he was seventeen, after suffering from severe arthritis. The practice proved more than efficacious: within a year he was symptom-free and was playing touch football every weekend.

I notice a bag full of marijuana sitting on the desk and ask if I can smell it. After Lotus nods I pick the bag up, unseal it, and inhale a loamy scent. 'Bush', I observe. 'How much do you charge for a bag of this?'

'Two [hundred and] eighty for an ounce', he says. 'Or $10 a gram'.

I ask him if he grows the weed himself and he replies, 'No. I source it from a local farmer'. He explains that he's also involved with two companies in Thailand to develop alternative seed stocks for the hemp food industry and for hemp fibre production, making two trips a year to confer with his overseas colleagues. When back in Byron Bay, he communicates and shares information via Facebook and email. Lotus tells me the main reason he sells pot nine hours a day, seven days a week, is to fund his research into the medicinal potential of marijuana. He estimates that he sells about 40 per cent of his product to recreational users, the profits of which allow him to give away the remaining 60 per cent to victims of cancer, arthritis, Parkinson's and multiple sclerosis. 'At the moment I'm developing a massage oil with a very high THC level to use on sufferers of cerebral palsy'.

Scrawled on the wall are dozens of phone numbers, handwritten in various colours of ink. And then I notice some graffiti, a quotation from Rumi: 'Out beyond ideas of wrongdoing, and rightdoing, there is a field. I'll meet you there.'

I ask Lotus if he's ever been arrested, and he rolls his eyes and nods. 'The last time was about two years ago. I got a section 9 and had to enter into a three-month merit course'. The program involved regular urine testing along with being educated on the long-term effects of drug abuse. 'During that time, my blood pressure went through the roof! My arresting officer reckoned I wouldn't make the three months, but I did'.

And how soon was it before he was back in the shop, smoking and dealing dope on a regular basis? Lotus laughs to himself and dries off yet another damp smiley-face sticker. 'About a week', he replies, shifting on the towel.

He tells me a story about a local pensioner named Chicken George, who'd retired from his government job in Sydney in the early '90s and had moved to Byron Bay. Chicken George, however, soon realised he had two problems: a growing taste for marijuana and an inability to live well on the old-age pension. 'So what he did was', says Lotus, 'at the start of every winter, he'd buy up a few kilos of weed, and then have his son – who owned a trucking business – remove the wheels of his van and store the dope in the tyres. Chicken George'd then drive up to Cairns on his own, check in to the Captain Cook Caravan Park, and spend two months dealing up there – which funded his lifestyle for the rest of the year'. Lotus adds that Chicken George did this for many winters, without being arrested, until his death four years ago at the age of seventy-eight.

'I do have one rule, though', says Lotus, 'and so did Chicken George. We don't sell to minors, no matter how much they offer to pay'.

***

One of the most recent trends developing among retirees, primarily on the Gold Coast, is to on-sell prescription drugs like painkiller oxycodone (nicknamed Hillbilly Heroin) to youths who like to party and mix them with alcohol. Older people can easily fake symptoms, they have immediate access to doctors, and due to pensioner discounts, their prescriptions are a fraction of the price of regular ones, ensuring a healthy profit for the elderly peddlers.

Mitchell Giles, CEO of Lives Lived Well, says that the idealisation of peaceful retirements by Australians belies a raft of problems faced by today's elderly – including isolation, depression and stress. 'These factors can strongly increase the likelihood of older people misusing alcohol or other drugs as a coping mechanism'. In fact, not only are many retirees trafficking drugs to assist them financially, some are also becoming unwitting addicts in the process. Figures from the Australian Institute of Health and Welfare show that between financial years 2003/4 and 2011/12 there was a 321.18 per cent increase in amphetamine use for Australians sixty years or older, while treatment for cannabis use among the over-sixties increased by 231.60 per cent.

However, it's not just the trafficking of cannabis and pills that is helping the elderly fund their retirements. In 2008, for example, Kevin Griffiths, then seventy-four, was still supplementing his fortnightly old-age pension cheque with the proceeds of dealing ice. He and his co-accused, Zivko Skepevski, sixty-seven, of Macquarie Hills, NSW, were allegedly the kingpins of one of the largest trafficking operations of the illegal drug ice uncovered by police in NSW. Police said the drugs they had seized as a result of the operation had a street value of $500 000 and were the equivalent of 10 000 single uses of the drug.

But Griffiths and Skepevski have not been the only Sydney-based pensioners making money out of crystal methamphetamine in the past few years.

On a sunny afternoon in Sydney I meet up for lunch with Don, an 83-year-old chemist who has been on a regular retainer for the past five years from a major Australian bikie gang. His only job is to develop alternative molecular structures for the production of crystal meth, ones that can evade the ever-changing federal laws.

We meet at an outdoor café, just around the corner from his unit in leafy Killarney Heights, where I find him perched over a takeaway coffee, a red recyclable shopping bag resting on his lap. His hair is cloud-white and styled into a curly pageboy cut, and he's sporting a black eye and bandaged wrist from a recent fall at home. Even though he's apparently unsteady on his feet these days, Don refuses to use a walking stick, let alone a Zimmer frame. With him is his friend Snapper, fifty, the middle-man between Don and the bikie gang, whose secondary, legitimate business is a pizza shop in Sydney's west.

In a soft, child-like voice Don remarks that it's impossible to make money in Australia by cooking up meth these days. 'Too many taxes (on the precursor drugs), and too much bureaucracy'.

'The chemicals are hard to get', adds Snapper. 'I mean on an industrial level'. Snapper has lost some of his front teeth and I have to lean forward to hear him fully. 'In the old days we used to be able to buy 200-litre drums of benzyl methyl ketone for fuck all—'

'And then all of a sudden you can only get 10-mil bottles!' interrupts Don, horrified.

For a few minutes Snapper and Don forget I'm here and begin to argue like an old married couple – not about what they're going to order for lunch – but over the correct names of various chemical combinations that they're experimenting with, including those concocted from a kangaroo-tanning product derived from ox blood.

'No', says the older man, shaking his head. 'It's phenyl acetic. I should know!'

Don explains that he flies to China three times a year, purchases precursor chemicals for a fraction of the price of those in Australia, and on-sells it to another international destination, after which time it will eventually arrive in Australia through a covert operation that he's not willing to discuss.

'So how does it all work?' I ask. 'I mean, between you and Snapper and the bikies? Who's in charge?'

The two men glance at each other and Don flips a white curl of hair over his shoulder, like a teenage girl preening herself in a mirror. 'It's easy', says Don. 'There's only one law'.

I lower my head and lean across the table.

'Whoever has the money', he continues, 'makes the rules'.

I'm reminded of Gina Rinehart's monopoly on the mining industry, and Rupert Murdoch's hold on international media, and can't help but smile. 'Not so different from any other business in Australia?'

Don smiles back like a naughty child and licks the milky froth from the lid of his coffee cup.

When I ask him about his background, he says that he was admitted to Melbourne University in the 1930s to study chemistry at the age of sixteen. An only child, both his parents were doctors and he served an apprenticeship with his father in order to receive his qualifications.

'How long was it before the apprentice outgrew the father?'

Don rolls his eyes. 'Oh, I was about twelve—' he replies, waving a dismissive hand.

Snapper lights a rollie and tells me that recently a Lebanese gang tried to move in on Don, also offering him a generous retainer in return for 'chemical consultations'. When members of the original bikie gang discovered what 'the Lebs' were up to, they directed two of their girlfriends to beat the interlopers up – which they did – right in front of their precious pensioner. The only problem was that the bikie chicks then moved in with Don for a few days, polished off his whisky, and used up all of his hospital-prescribed Xanax, Valium and morphine.

Developing alternative strains of crystal meth, however, is not Don's only preoccupation. 'I've also experimented with diet drugs … Synthetic skin—'

'Tell her about the Viagra', adds Snapper.

Don nods and explains that a few years ago he was involved in the making of a topical form of Viagra – an ointment rather than a pill. He used one of his drinking buddies at a local pub as a guinea pig, but the medication only partly worked.

'He disappeared into the men's room to rub it on. But when he came back five minutes later he wasn't happy', says Don.

'Why's that?' I asked. 'Were there side effects?'

Don laughs. 'He didn't get a hard-on, but the ointment made his fingers stiff—'

Snapper snorts. '—the poor bastard couldn't pick up his glass anymore and so he had to drink his beer through a straw!'

As our laughter dies down the waitress approaches but I manage to wave her away.

'What are the other challenges for you when manufacturing meth', I ask both men, 'besides sourcing the chemicals?'

'It takes three people a week to cook one batch up—'

'—glassware,' overlaps Snapper. 'Sometimes we buy it second-hand from an internet firm—'

'Yes, but even second-hand glass has to be registered with the government', adds a withering Don.

'Like an art work with a provenance?'

He nods sullenly.

Snapper sighs and rubs his two-day growth. 'But it's just a code of practice – not a law. Nothin' we can't deal with'.

The waitress, standing in the doorway, glances at her watch. She approaches us again, puts the lunch menus on the table, and disappears.

'I'm not eating today', declares Don.

'That's what you said yesterday', Snapper reminds him.

'I'll eat tomorrow, instead'.

'You said that yesterday, too'.

Snapper tells me that the reason Don was freed from remand

in Pentridge a few years ago was because he'd become too popular with his much younger prison mates. 'He was like an old grandpa teaching them all how to cook. The screws got so mad they had to kick him out before he totally corrupted them all!'

As Don rummages in his red shopping bag, I ask him if he ever uses the drugs he's obviously so skilled at developing. He shakes his head, uninterested, and continues rummaging. 'So is it the money?' I add, wondering aloud why he'd risk so much to provide for an infamous and dangerous bikie gang. He laughs briefly and pulls out a notebook. 'The money's good, but that's not all'.

'Well, what is it then?' I persist. 'The company? The sense of risk?'

He looks at me directly with his good eye and hands me his business card: Don Miller: Consulting Chemist; Chemical Analysis; Custom Synthesis.

He grins and places a plump hand on mine. 'It's nothing more than to satisfy my boundless curiosity'.

Girls Gone Wild

(2013)

'If we get into a fight', says Jamie, 'you're not gonna call the cops on us, are you?' I'm sitting in the living room of a hostel for homeless Aboriginal women and children in Sydney's west, talking to two young self-confessed 'bad bitches' who in 2011 were charged with carjacking and larceny.

Jamie and Leeyah, eighteen and seventeen at the time respectively, along with another teenage girl, were crossing a road on their way to meet their drug dealer in Toongabbie when they spotted a woman parking her car and, more importantly, the handbag on her lap. Leeyah lunged at the open window, grabbed the handbag and pulled the driver from the car. She then jumped behind the wheel and threw the bag on the floor while Jamie leaped into the passenger side and the third girl dove into the back. They took off at high speed down the laneway, careened around a corner and onto a main street.

For the next two-and-a-half weeks they joy-rode through outer Sydney, buying and using drugs and accidentally hitting telegraph poles and garbage bins. The girls were finally caught when a drunk relative crashed the car near a breathalyser unit.

Jamie and Leeyah have agreed to meet me to discuss their lives and the perceived rise of underage violence and gang activities among Australian girls. According to NSW Bureau of Crime

57

Statistics data, the number of juvenile female offenders soared by 36 per cent in the decade to June 2009, compared with an 8 per cent increase for juvenile males.

There's anecdotal evidence, too. In September 2011, YouTube clips of pre-arranged brawls between girls as young as fourteen in Sydney's south-west went viral and were reported throughout the world. The same year, four girls, aged fourteen and fifteen, bashed and robbed a 26-year-old woman in Sydney's south-east while she was waiting for a bus. In 2013, two fourteen-year-old girls attempted to rob a man on a Sydney train by punching him in the face and burning his head with a lit cigarette. The same week, two more girls, aged sixteen and seventeen, tried to hold up a man at Lakemba train station with a pair of fake guns.

I'm especially curious about this phenomenon because as a teenager I lived in a Public Housing estate in Carlton, Melbourne, with an alcoholic single mother, after having been on the run for a year – and through three states – from my violent stepfather. During that time, I got into drugs (cocaine, marijuana, LSD), did a fair bit of shoplifting, and was busted once for writing graffiti. But it never occurred to me to join a group of other girls and attack a stranger for money or other possessions. As a fifteen-year-old, if I needed cash I did it the traditional way: babysitting, cleaning houses, teaching children to swim.

***

'I just wanna know', says a slim woman in her early forties, leaning against the doorjamb of the hostel's living room and folding her arms, 'are you undercover or what?' This is Jamie's mother, who also lives in the hostel. I have to stop myself from laughing. 'If I were an undercover cop', I answer, 'do you think I'd tell you?' After giving me a dismissive once-over, she nods to her daughter and disappears down the hall.

Jamie's face has a girlish gentleness, but when I ask her where she grew up and where she went to school, her expression clouds. 'I grew up in DOCS [Department of Family and Community Services]', she confesses. 'I grew up all over'.

In foster homes?

She nods and explains that her three sisters also grew up in state care. She looks into her lap and fiddles with her mobile. 'I only met my real mother three years ago'.

Jamie tells me that when she was thirteen she was released into the care of an aunt. In a Faginesque twist, a relative forced her to shoplift. As a consequence, Jamie ran away from home and lived with an uncle for three weeks before he was arrested and jailed for drug abuse. By the time she was sixteen, she had been placed with a foster family at Kemps Creek, but only lasted three days before running away yet again, ending up in the care of another relative who, she says, also demanded that she shoplift and steal.

As Jamie talks, her breathing grows short and she becomes agitated, pulling on her ponytail, turning the phone in her hands, as if she's reliving a time she'd rather forget. She met her closest ally, cousin Leeyah, three years ago, and since then they've become inseparable. During that short time they've also managed to get into an extraordinary amount of trouble together.

'It usually happens when we want to get on [pot]', explains Leeyah. 'We're okay if we can have a cone first thing in the morning, but if we can't we get really stressed and that's usually when we tend to get violent'.

When I ask about details of the carjacking two years ago, Leeyah's eyes widen and she shoots me a cheeky grin. 'We don't just rob anyone', she replies, shaking her head. 'Like, we wouldn't have stolen the car if there'd been a baby in the back, or if it'd been an old person driving'.

She pauses and crosses her arms: 'We do have ethics, you know!'

Leeyah goes on to tell me that she grew up on a Public Housing estate with seventeen siblings in Sydney's west and has convictions dating back to the age of twelve, when she attempted to rob a woman at an ATM. Since then, she has been in and out of juvenile detention centres for various crimes, including theft, assault, and intimidating a police officer. 'People think juvenile detention is a bad influence on kids, but really it's a fucking paradise!' When Leeyah smiles, her face glows with a sepia-toned beauty. 'There's swimming pools, sports ovals, nice rooms ...'

Her eyes flicker around the hostel's pale grey walls. I lean forward. 'So did you keep committing crimes so you could go back to juvie?'

She laughs to herself and nods. 'Course! Who'd ever want to leave there? It's a fucking paradise!'

It's now 5pm and the hostel's dinner bell has rung. As I prepare to leave I ask them both what they think will happen to them beyond this – living day to day at the hostel, carjacking and rolling people for money. The girls fall quiet for a few moments and the gale outside rattles the windowpanes.

'I think I'll end up in jail', Leeyah finally admits, without a trace of self-pity.

I suggest that there seems to be only two options for girls in her situation – going to jail, or getting pregnant and getting into the system that way.

Leeyah glances across at Jamie and briefly smiles. 'And I think you'll be the one who'll get pregnant', she says, pointing at her cousin. Jamie thinks for a moment, grins shyly, and agrees.

***

It would be easy to assume that the rise of underage female crime is limited to Sydney and Melbourne, but smaller cities and regional areas have become just as dangerous. In 2008, for example, 39-year-old mother-of-three Tanya Rowe died as a result of being bashed by a gang of girls outside a Perth railway station. Another attack and robbery occurred in May 2011, also at a Perth station, after one gang member stole a woman's handbag and the twenty or so others turned on the victim, dragging her to the ground by her hair and punching and kicking her face and body, leaving her with a shattered cheekbone and missing teeth. And in 2010, Newcastle police were hunting a group of girls nicknamed 'the Pyjama Gang', who were sneaking out at night in their dressing gowns and slippers to roll women for money and phones.

In the northern NSW town of Casino in 2008, a gang of five girls attacked then seventeen-year-old Julie-Anne Gill one Friday night. In spite of a police highway patrol car passing during the beginning of the incident, and two security guards watching on from the nightclub across the road, Gill was pushed to the ground, dragged along the road and kicked and punched for twenty minutes. As a result, she sustained a black eye, fractured nose, chipped tooth, skinned legs and ripped toenails.

'It still affects me every day', the mother of two tells me over the phone. 'For a while afterwards I slept in my mother's bed with her. I had nightmares. It took me two years before I could walk downtown on my own. Even now, I'm still scared'. What made the attack even worse, she adds in a shaky voice, was that it occurred only twelve weeks after her father had passed away.

Gill believes that in her case the attack was random and possibly a case of mistaken identity. 'A lot of kids do it because they're bored – because there's nothing to do in the town'. She tells me that two weeks after she was bashed, another gang of girls attacked two of her closest friends outside the Casino Golf Club, knocking out several teeth from one of them before stealing their purses and mobile phones.

She agrees that some of the problems are due to slack parenting and underage drinking, but for her the situation is much more complicated. 'Here in Casino we don't have a police force on the weekends. If there's any trouble we've got to call the cops in Lismore [30 kilometres away] and half the time they don't even turn up'.

She adds that many residents of the town, when reporting a crime, are often forced to exaggerate the severity of an incident in order to be taken seriously by the Lismore police. 'They keep doing it because they can get away with it', she says. 'There's no authority'.

***

When I tell the Melbourne taxi driver I want to go to the suburb of Sunshine, the first thing he asks me is, 'Why?' He says he rarely takes fares to or from Sunshine because he's been robbed too many times. 'By teenage girls?' I ask. He nods and adjusts the rear-view mirror. 'Once they get close to home they just jump out of the cab and run!'

I've heard it said that Sunshine is so beset with violent teenage girls that housewives now carry two handbags when they catch the train – one for their belongings and one to give up in case they're robbed. And Sunshine is far from being the only troubled Melbourne suburb. As we drive up Flemington Road, I remember reading about a 34-year-old woman who, in February 2010, was assaulted and robbed at knifepoint by two teenage girls while waiting for a bus outside Glenroy railway station. As the cab swings through Footscray, past gaudy graffiti and the long shadows of Public Housing high rises, I also recall that, last year, a gang of four girls attacked seventeen-year-old Chantelle Papi in Fawkner before stealing her credit cards, mobile phone and identification.

University of Tasmania criminologist Professor Rob White, who in 2013 published the book *Youth Gangs, Violence and Social Respect*, argues that most of what the media reports about female teenage violence in Australia is not related to gang activity in the conventional sense (initiations, tattoos, tags and territorialism), but is more a result of loose-knit groups of girlfriends and/or relations who enjoy getting into trouble.

White maintains that, for some young women, fighting is indeed 'a regular part of their street experience [and] motivated by excitement, status and protection', adding that 'over half of all female appearances in juvenile court are related to acts intended to cause injury or theft'.

In a laneway near Sunshine railway station, a boom box blares rap music as teenage boys spray graffiti. A group of Sudanese teenage girls, with long, egret-like legs, pauses to watch them. The suburb is a stew of ethnicities and businesses: discount variety stores, African dress shops, tattoo parlours, tobacco outlets, Vietnamese sweet stores and pawn shops. Suddenly a toddler appears wearing pink gumboots. Holding a toy mobile phone, she's intrigued by the rap music and begins to dance in circles. Her young, pregnant mother struggles past, pushing a stroller against the wind. Inside lies a baby with a chocolate-ringed mouth and watery blue eyes.

While the toddler continues to dance, I chat with the mother, Tanya. She admits that as a teenager she fell in with the wrong crowd through a boyfriend and got into hard drugs. Now, at twenty-eight, she has three children under nine, two stepchildren, and a baby due in six weeks time. The irony is that she has become terrified of the very same kind of teenagers she once embraced.

She tells me that, just before Christmas 2012, she was walking out of a store with her kids when a group of teenage girls slammed the baby's stroller over, with the infant still inside, and made off with the baby bag that had been hanging from the handle. When police found and returned the discarded bag the next day, everything was missing: $100, an heirloom ring, and the toddler's clothes, disposable nappies and formula.

As her daughter continues to dance, Tanya lights a Longbeach. She tells me that last year she was waiting with her kids on a platform at the railway station when her eight-year-old daughter walked into the public toilet and accidentally interrupted two teen-age girls shooting up heroin outside the stalls. The teenagers first began verbally abusing the daughter for 'fucking up their fit' and pushed her outside. When Tanya attempted to intervene, the girls slammed her up against a wall and threatened to bash her sense-less unless she compensated them for the heroin they'd accidentally spilled. While they continued to threaten and rough up Tanya, the quick-thinking eight-year-old grabbed the baby stroller, ran down the platform with it, out of harm's way, and used her mother's mobile to call triple zero.

Now, as the toddler continues to dance to the booming rap music, waving her fake mobile like a fairy wand, I can imagine her in about ten years time, trawling the same lanes and streets, still intrigued by music and mobile phones, but no longer so fresh-faced and innocent.

The following day I meet youth worker Les Twentyman in a café overlooking Whitten Oval in Footscray. The offices of his foun-dation, the 20th Man Fund [now The Les Twentyman Foundation], are just down the road, and were established over two decades ago to provide social services for Melbourne's troubled teens.

With his white hair and beard, Twentyman looks more like a grandfather who could double as Santa Claus than a tireless worker trawling Melbourne's streets at night, helping the young, the vio-lent, the drug-addicted and the abused. 'The problems [of violent girls] often stem from homelessness', says Twentyman, gazing over the empty sports field. 'These girls are often getting abused at home, in so many ways – it could be incest or parents on crack or whatever – and running away, getting into gangs and drugs … well, living like that is often better, for them, than being abused at home'.

He tells me that earlier this year he reunited a formerly home-less fifteen-year-old girl with her mother and stepfather, after the parents had passed all safety checks with DOCS and other ser-vices. But the girl only remained with them for a few days before running away again. Twentyman recently discovered the reason for the second disappearance: the mother and stepfather had established an unlicensed brothel in the home and expected the daughter to service clients.

He tells me that there are three main girl gangs currently operating in Melbourne, the Lavs (from the suburb of Laverton), the West Sides and the Dun-bees: 'The Lavs are all Pacific Islander girls who are having trouble transitioning from primary school to high school, the West Sides are a gang who bash up any girls who dare to go out with any of their ex-boyfriends, and a couple of years ago Dun-bees were involved in the stabbing of two people in Sunshine'.

All three groups appear to have emerged from established male gangs. I've noticed, however, some crucial differences between the male and female gang members. Male gang members are usually aged between seventeen and twenty-six; they brawl with machetes, bottles, poles, knuckle-dusters and knives; and most admit that riots and fights arise because they are protecting their 'territories'. Members of girl gangs, on the other hand, can be as young as twelve, usually don't use dangerous weapons, and prefer attacking victims by punching, kicking and hair-pulling. Their prime motivation, it seems, is not protecting their 'area', like the males, but stealing for materialistic reasons.

Nearly all of these girls come from disadvantaged areas. They don't have much power and enjoy very little respect from the wider community. They're also bombarded daily with images and narratives promoting materialism and excess, yet they have little access to the wealth they witness. Hence the obsession with beating up older, more affluent women and stealing possessions that will earn them peer respect: cars, cash, handbags and mobiles.

Twentyman scoops his phone from the table and begins stabbing the keys. After a brief 'Hello', he hands the mobile over to me and I find myself talking to Detective Superintendent Pat Boyle, a deep-voiced man who has been in the force for several decades and is completing a Master's thesis on Melbourne gang activity. 'A lot of guys in gangs will use their girlfriends – that's how they get involved', he says. 'They get them to carry the drugs and the guns, 'cause the guys think it's safer'.

***

In Darwin a few years ago, a gang of teenage girls attacked four young women in Smith Street Mall, with one victim being dragged by her hair along the pavement while others kicked her in the back and their male friends stood back and watched. And in 2010, two teenage girls and a twenty-year-old man from Casino took turns to stab a man six times in the car park of a tourist lookout near Kyogle. The three also filmed the torture on their mobile phones before rolling the wounded man over an embankment.

Detective Boyle tells me that when the police are confronted by gangs of both boys and girls in Melbourne, 'the girls are the most violent, especially when they're drunk. They like showing off in front of their boyfriends'.

When I enquire about the potential benefits of juvenile detention – counselling, health and education services – Boyle is not enthusiastic. 'Though there are systems in place to rehabilitate youth, there is still a need for the individual to make the most of those opportunities, and there can be peer group pressure that upsets those with potential for change. This is also no different outside those environments'.

I ask Twentyman what might be done to assist girls who get into trouble at such a premature age. He fixes me with a hard, blue-eyed stare: 'We've got to start dealing with these girls as victims rather than locking them up all the time'.

He goes on to explain that the baby bonus – currently at $5000 for the first child – has not helped the plight of vulnerable young women. 'There's the old cliché of teenage mums splurging on flat-screen TVs, but most of the time, in this kind of culture, it's the boyfriend who takes the $5000 bonus and blows it all on drugs'.

Twentyman hands me his phone again and I find myself talking to sixteen-year-old Crystal, who joined the Dun-bees gang at age thirteen and spent a couple of years with them. Expecting to hear a voice cracked and corrupted by her experiences, I'm shocked to hear instead what seems like a soft-voiced seven-year-old who has suddenly found herself lost in a fairground.

Crystal says that when she was a member, the gang consisted of about ten girls, all aged between thirteen and fourteen. 'We used to just get really drunk', she confesses. 'And then we'd go into the city and bash and rob people'.

Twentyman explains that Crystal had a violent upbringing and that her mother is a former heroin addict. 'These days, lots of kids are growing up around hard drugs in the home', he says. 'It becomes normal. Then they stop going to school and start getting into trouble'.

During 2013, more than 2000 children were expelled from schools in Melbourne's western suburbs, but Twentyman is adamant that punishing kids by refusing them an education is neither effective nor fair, and he cites the 56 per cent unemployment rate of teenagers aged fifteen to nineteen in Melbourne's north-west.

'I'd also recommend the introduction of compulsory national service for teenagers not in school or being employed', he adds. 'Not for military training, but to gain life skills, job skills, and to improve their self-esteem'.

***

Back in Sydney, I meet Jamie and Leeyah to have their pictures taken. As the photographer sets up the camera in a lane by the railway, I ask Jamie if she'd been abused during her years in foster care. She flicks her hair back and nods. 'I had to clean their houses for them. Babysit for them. Steal for some of them. I was treated like a slave', she says, shivering in the wind. 'A slave', she adds for emphasis.

She admits she was fortunate in that she was never sexually abused in care, but when I ask how many foster homes she's grown up in, her eyes are suddenly glazed and remote. She finally shakes her head. 'There's been so many. I can't remember'.

As a train roars above us, I decide to change the subject: 'Do you have any plans for the weekend?'

Her eyebrows do a little dance. 'Shake and take', she murmurs. 'On the trains?'

'Yeah, well, we have to', she replies. 'We need to get some yarny [marijuana] and everything we've got is in hock at the moment'.

When two Asian women amble up the lane and begin to pass us, Jamie can't help herself – she reaches out playfully and touches the large purse one of them is carrying. The woman reels away, terrified, not realising that Jamie at this moment is only horsing around. I find it a telling piece of improvised acting on Jamie's part, demonstrating to me how easy it is for her to snatch a bag and get away with it.

I ask Leeyah if jail is better than juvenile detention. 'Jail's m-a-a-a-d, eh?' she replies enthusiastically. She admits that she didn't even mind being in isolation for two weeks, her punishment for having 'hit a screw'. 'There was only a shower and a bed and I was only allowed out for an hour a day. But they let me draw in isolation – that's what I like doing, drawing – and I could also smoke in the cell, so I didn't care'.

Leeyah also tells me she got into trouble after the marijuana supply in the prison dried up. 'I made a deal with one of the gardeners: I traded tobacco for a can of petrol that I could sniff'. She was busted after displaying manic behaviour and reeking of fumes, ending up in isolation yet again.

As the girls shiver in the westerly wind and stare down the lens of the camera, I think back to my teenage years. My mother may have been single, alcoholic and living in Public Housing, but she always had dinner on the table at 6pm, made sure I went to school, encouraged me in my desire to write, and never failed to let me know that I was loved. I eventually grew out of that rebellious stage and by the age of seventeen began to study visual art, instead.

Purple-black clouds are massing above us and there's the smell of rain in the air. A car drives up the lane towards us. 'Watch this', says Jamie, as she moves directly in front of it. 'You watch, the locks'll go straight down'.

And of course she's right: as soon as the female Asian driver glimpses the figure of Jamie blocking her way, the windows shoot up and door locks thump down. There's a stand-off for about two minutes; the driver's too scared to get out and confront her and Jamie's enjoying herself too much to bother moving.

It's only when the woman's face tightens into an exasperated scowl, when we see her silently curse and thump the steering wheel, that Jamie gives way. She slowly backs off and, as the terrified driver slams down the accelerator, Jamie leaps onto the footpath and begins to laugh.

Elsie Turns Forty

(2014)

'I've been bitten, had my ribs broken, and my back's been kicked so badly I can't feel my spine'. She glances out the window and shudders. 'It started on our honeymoon and lasted all of twenty-two years'.

I'm sitting in Elsie Women's Refuge with Marie, forty-five, who has just fled her violent husband. Perched beside her on the couch are Sophia, nineteen, and Lucy, fifteen, also victims of their father's ongoing abuse. I'm here because it's the fortieth anniversary of the opening of Elsie, the first refuge of its kind in Australia to provide urgent assistance to battered wives and children.

As a child, I myself was sheltered here in 1976, after my stepfather had beaten my mother and me badly and had voiced plans to drop my baby brother into a bucket of boiling water. By this time, he'd been abusing and threatening to kill us for three years and there'd been nowhere to turn: neighbours, clergy, and even the police refused to get involved in what they presumed were merely domestic disputes. And four decades later, I'm curious to find out how the refuge began, what has changed socially and politically, and what, if anything, has remained the same.

***

By 2014, there were 300 such refuges around Australia, but back in early 1974, the only place abused women and children could find temporary shelter was at a Salvation Army facility, which provided a bed for the night but banned traumatised families from residing there during the day, and provided no health, legal or social services. Due to the lack of financial and moral support, most women ended up returning to violent homes.

At the time, 29-year-old feminist Anne Summers was a post-graduate student at Sydney University when she happened to see a film by Erin Pizzey, based on Pizzey's book *Scream Quietly or the Neighbours Will Hear*, which highlighted the extent of domestic violence in England. After a two-day Women's Commission Conference, plans were made to start a refuge in Sydney.

Summers was aware of Chiswick Women's Shelter in London, the first of its kind in the world, and phoned the shelter to ask for advice. 'I'll never forget it,' says Summers, now in her seventies, sitting in the dining room of her Potts Point terrace. 'There were kids screaming in the background – all kinds of noise – and when I asked the woman on the line how to set up a refuge, she replied, emphatically, "Just do it!"'

The first challenge for the group was to find premises. One night Summers was watching *Four Corners* on ABC TV when she saw a segment about the Church of England planning to sell hundreds of unoccupied Glebe houses to the government for Public Housing, a consequence of the Green Ban era's devotion to saving historic homes for the underprivileged. A former squatter, Summers was well aware of the then prevailing squatters' rights, and scouted around Glebe until she found an unoccupied cottage in sound condition on Westmoreland Street. The original sign near the door proclaimed the house was named 'Elsie'.

A few days later Summers and fourteen other women, armed with shovels and broomsticks, marched down to the appointed cottage, smashed a window, and broke in. 'The next thing we did was change the locks. And then we called the media'.

She remembers giving interviews from the front yard of Elsie: 'I was wearing a pair of blue denim overalls – there were news cameras everywhere. And then there was this one journo, Michael Moore, who said, in all seriousness, "But don't the women ask for it?"'

Today, the question seems so anachronistic that we both begin to laugh. In his reaction, however, it soon became obvious that Moore was part of an unpopular minority: the level of support given to the refuge by the wider community was nothing less than phenomenal. John Laws interviewed Summers on his radio program and announced the phone number of the refuge multiple times, leading to the first arrivals of battered women and children. White goods wholesaler Joyce Mayne rang up, asked what the refuge required, and the next day delivered refrigerators and washing machines. Rotary obliged by securing the back fence and supplying playground equipment for the children. Local shopkeepers gave them leftover produce.

It would be a year, however, before the refuge would receive any form of funding. 'So how did you raise actual money during that time?' I make a joke about the women running cake stalls and setting up kissing booths.

Summers smiles and shakes her head. 'Well, I dealt marijuana for that year – that's how we got the cash!' She explains why the locals at that time always preferred to buy her cannabis: 'Because it was *Elsie* pot. It was politically correct!'

It was Summers' colleague, Diana Beaton, who was ultimately responsible for securing government support. 'In February 1975, Diana was attending an ALP conference in Terrigal. Now, I have to say, Diana was absolutely stunning – no man could take his eyes off her. So she goes to the conference dinner and she finds herself sitting next to Bill Hayden. Bill probably couldn't believe his luck – being seated next to such a beautiful young woman. But to his surprise, all Diana wanted to talk about all night was funding for women's refuges. And that night she convinced him to at least visit Elsie to see what it was like'.

Summers recalls Hayden's arrival: 'He decided to park his car around the corner, and turn up unannounced – probably thinking he could catch us out and unprepared. After Hayden knocked on the door, one of the resident mothers answered and told him he couldn't come in because men were banned from the refuge. "But I'm Bill Hayden", he explained, "the minister for social services—."'

'"I don't care who you are", replied the mother. "No men are allowed!" She slammed the door in his face and Hayden began walking off down the street, when one of the workers recognised him, ran after him, and dragged him back.'

After our laughter dies down, Summers adds, in a lower voice, 'He was appalled at what he saw ... he realised just by walking through those few rooms, seeing those women, meeting them, seeing the kids. He said, "I'll do anything."'

After she sips some water, she asks, 'Have you heard about the latest problem with Elsie?'

When I shake my head Summers explains that there is a possibility that from this year [2014] the state and federal funding of the refuge could be put out for general tender, meaning that the company with the lowest tender will be given authority to operate the facility, essentially undermining the original feminist ideology of the refuge. 'That means that men could not only be allowed to stay at the refuge, they could also be running it, as well'.

The idea, to me, seems ridiculous and possibly dangerous. I remind Summers of employment ads for positions in Indigenous communities, whereby a condition of employment, due to cultural sensitivities, is that the applicant be of Aboriginal or Torres Strait Islander descent. 'Why can't the same sensitivities be applied to abused and traumatised women and children?' I ask.

Summers purses her lips and shrugs. 'It's the general way things are going these days'.

***

'My partner didn't beat me up', says Polly, a short, thin, pale-faced woman in her mid-thirties, who is sitting in the back garden of the refuge, drinking tea. 'It was emotional abuse and sexual abuse'. Polly and her two children, six and three, have been staying at Elsie for several months, after her partner forced her to return from interstate to resolve access issues with regard to his daughter, the three-year-old.

'When I first fell pregnant, he didn't want the kid, and we broke up'. She adds that it was only after she gave birth that he began making promises. 'He was very charming, and he wanted us to be a family'.

Unfortunately, Polly had to undergo a caesarean birth and during the operation, part of her bowel was severed, causing further complications and infections. In the following two years she would have four more operations, which almost cost her her life several times.

'As soon as he moved in with me, after the birth, that's when the abuse began'.

'When you say sexual abuse', I ask, leaning forward. 'Do mean rape?'

Polly swallows nervously and nods. 'He's six foot four. I'd come out of hospital, right after surgery, already with internal injuries, and he'd hold me down on the floor and restrain me, and then he'd rape me – repeatedly – and I was still wearing a colostomy bag!'

Like many abused women, Polly was never sure what would 'set her partner off' and she was always walking on eggshells and trying to pre-empt his mood swings. She explains that many times he's shaken her son so vigorously that her son has pissed himself; her daughter has returned from access visits with unexplained bruises on her arms and legs. Once, he arranged for couples counselling so Polly could 'better understand his needs'. One day when he was driving them to a session he was so disgruntled about the counsellor, who'd begun focusing on his problems rather than Polly's, that he tried to kill them both by attempting to drive off the Harbour Bridge. 'I grabbed the steering wheel just before we hit the barrier. He jumped out of the car and ran away. Then I slammed on the handbrake'. On another occasion, she adds, he tried to drive the car straight into a building.

When I raise with Polly the possibility that the operations of the refuge could soon be put out to tender, which could lead to men not only staying at the refuge, but also running it, too, Polly bristles and shakes her head. 'No! No way. I wouldn't be here if men were running it'. She tells me that it took her weeks to even begin to trust the female workers. 'I was in counselling for about a month with Roberta before I could admit to her – and even to myself – that I'd been raped. Up until that point, I'd been in denial'.

She pulls out her mobile and begins showing me photos of her daughter's bruised limbs. Some clearly show a pattern of five brownish marks, the size of $2 coins, where someone has obviously dug their fingers into her flesh.

'Have you shown the police these?' I ask.

She nods wearily and briefly closes her eyes. 'They told me that I had a victim mentality and was just being melodramatic'.

***

It's an odd feeling meeting a stranger who's responsible for saving your life.

I'm sitting at an outdoor café opposite Diana Beaton, now in her seventies, whom Summers credits with securing initial funding for Elsie in 1975, only a year before my mother, baby brother and I fetched up there in the middle of the night.

When I tell Beaton this story, she smiles sadly and nods. She's a slim, graceful woman with short curly hair and a clear-eyed face straight out of a Renoir painting. She tells me that in the early days of Elsie, when they were still squatting, she performed what she called 'home rescues', which were more like improvised military operations. One day in 1974 she received a call from a woman in Newtown who was desperate to escape an abusive relationship. 'Come and get me now,' urged the woman, 'while he's not here'. Beaton turned up at the given address alone and without protection, and helped the woman throw her few possessions into garbage bags. Just as they were about to leave, however, the woman's husband appeared on the front verandah. 'We grabbed the bags, ran out into the backyard, and began throwing the bags over the fence', recalls a still-stunned Beaton. 'I managed to crawl up the fence, too, and pulled the woman up with me, just as her husband was opening the back door. We ran for our lives and grabbed a cab'.

Like Summers, Beaton is still amused by her own naïveté and that of the other founding members: 'We had no training. And the perception by the Whitlam government was that we were a bunch of middle-class women helping other middle-class women get out of their marriages'. In 1974, as a consequence of the Hayden visit, Elsie received a one-off grant of $24 000 to fund six positions for a twelve-month period. The biggest task for the collective, however, would be to convince the government that domestic violence was a social issue rather than a health issue, and that an abusive relationship could be found just as easily in the gated mansions of Vaucluse as in the slums of Redfern.

By June 1975, there were eight women's refuges scattered around the country, all operating on scant budgets and uncertain future funding. Beaton recalls that it was Lyndall Ryan, from the office of women's affairs, who urged her to ring around the other refuges and 'get some figures on how many families come through'.

Beaton stirs her tea, obviously still shocked by what she uncovered. She catches her breath and glances up at the sky. 'I couldn't believe it: over an eighteen-month period, we'd sheltered 13 500 women and children – even we were gobsmacked'.

After the figures were submitted to the government, the then minister for urban and regional development, Tom Uren, also visited Elsie. At the time, the residents were still squatting under Dickensian conditions: the refuge was flooded and was ankle-deep in water; there was only one toilet; and some of the kids had come down with giardia lamblia, a stomach parasite often caused by poor hygiene.

Lyndall Ryan had predicted to Beaton that if the government decided to fund Elsie, it would also have to fund the seven other refuges, and fortunately she was right. Not long after the Uren visit, the collective first read in the paper that triennial funding had been approved for all eight facilities.

'That was the turning point', says Beaton, smiling.

***

By 2014 there were more than 300 women's refuges around Australia, with a mix of state and federal funding, and all a consequence of the activism of a handful of feminists in 1974. Those four decades saw many changes, mostly due to education and technology: the White Ribbon movement, for example, established in Australian in 2003, is an ongoing male-led campaign to end violence against women; instead of pleading with a taxi driver or a police officer for directions to a given refuge, as my mother had, for example, an abused woman or child can call a domestic violence hotline and receive immediate assistance; CCTV cameras are also placed in vital areas of all refuges for added security from vengeful partners; each refuge works closely with various social services to transition mothers and children into safer environments; and Telstra has granted free silent numbers for relocated victims of violence. Since 2012, 'SOS' personal alarms have become available to keep vulnerable women safe from former partners who threaten them with serious injury or death. The alarms are provided to those who have an apprehended violence order or are in the process of obtaining one. When activated, the call for help is prioritised by police. The device has a GPS to guide police to the victim's location.

'Yes, but technology can also work against the victims', argues Tanya Smith, a manager of Elsie and herself a survivor of a violent marriage. 'For example, a husband can secretly plant a GPS in his wife's car and follow her around – even after she's left him, or thought she has'. We also discuss the Simon Gittany courtroom drama, in which it was revealed that the jealous, paranoid partner monitored fiancée Lisa Harnum's movements via hidden cameras planted in and around the apartment they shared, before throwing her to her death, in a fit of rage, from their fifteenth-floor balcony in July 2011. Texting, and social media sites such as Facebook, Twitter and Instagram, can also diminish the anonymity required to establish a new life. Technology may provide a fast means of escape, but it also increases the chance that the escape will be short-lived.

Residents of Elsie, mother Marie and daughters Sophia and Lucy, know only too well the dangers of technology when it comes to dealing with domestic violence. Marie, for example, was forbidden to contact her family and friends without her husband Lorne's permission, a rule he enforced by regularly checking her mobile phone. What made it harder for Marie was that she and Lorne also worked together running their own antique store, without any other staff, for over twenty years, increasing her sense of isolation. 'He'd lose his temper, drag me into the office, shut the door, and kick me, punch me, and pull my hair out. And after it was over, I'd have to clean myself up, put on some make up, and walk back into the shop to deal with the customers'.

I ask the girls if Lorne also abused them and they both look down in their laps and nod sadly. Sophia confesses that she recently read a diary entry written when she was only eight years old: *I wish Dad would let me read books that I like, like picture books, but if I do I know he'll bite me and bash me, just like he always does.*

When I ask if there was a defining moment or action that caused Marie to decide to leave for good, the three of them grow anxious and begin talking over one another in high, breathless voices.

Finally, the youngest, Lucy loudly wins out. 'I remember saying to Mum one day, when she and Sophia had to go to an appointment, "Whatever you do, don't leave me alone with Dad"'. Mother and sister were perturbed by the admission, but since the appointment was urgent and couldn't be changed, the two reluctantly left Lucy at home. During their absence Lorne complained bitterly about Lucy's behaviour. 'He didn't think I was practising the piano enough'.

I wait for Lucy to continue, but she falters. 'So what happened then?' I ask. 'Did he hurt you?'

She nods, blinking back tears.

Her mother's hand suddenly flies to her face, as if she's blocking a punch. Marie explains that this year Lucy, for the first time in her life, began failing her classes and skipping school, and had already packed her bags in a plan to run away from home forever.

Up until this point in the conversation, mother and daughters have been remarkably stoic, but when I turn to Lucy and ask her how her father had hurt her during the day she'd been left alone, she begins sobbing uncontrollably. 'He threw me down on the floor, smashed my head against the piano, and dragged me around the room by my hair'. I can tell by the startled reactions of the other two that this is the first time Lucy has detailed to them the extent of Lorne's abuse. Her older sister puts an arm around her and Marie's face is so wreathed with pain and regret she can barely utter the following words: 'That's what made me want to leave', she says in a trembling voice. 'I chose to be with Lorne, but these girls didn't.

I didn't want Lucy to end up as a prostitute on the street just because of the choices I'd made'.

But technology almost derailed their disappearance: Marie tells me that Lorne spent over a month cyberstalking them, hacking into his daughters' Facebook accounts for a hint of their whereabouts, trawling the internet for a mention of his wife's name, until he finally tracked her down to an antique store in Sydney's east where she'd found some temporary work. Marie noticed him standing in front of the store one afternoon, and walked outside to confront him. The two spent three hours arguing on the street – with Lorne promising to buy her jewellery from Tiffany's and to take her on a European holiday, if only she and the girls would come home. When Marie refused he insisted that he drive her back to wherever she was now living, which she also declined. Lorne followed her to the train station as she was making her way back to the refuge. The only way Marie could prevent him from boarding the train was by threatening to call the police.

***

Anne Summers believes that there've been many advances in how we deal with domestic abuse – the proliferation of refuges around the country; free silent numbers for victims; stronger laws, including the use of AVOs – but when I suggest the underlying violent behaviour hasn't changed that much, she shakes her head. 'No, it hasn't changed at all', she says. 'In fact, it's worse!' I mention that popular, contemporary drugs like crystal methamphetamine, ketamine, and others, non-existent in 1974, and which can trigger aggressive, psychotic episodes, have contributed to the escalating violence, and she agrees.

Current data reports that over their lifetime, about one in three Australian women will experience physical violence and about one in five will experience some form of sexual violence. Aboriginal and Torres Strait Islander women, and women with a disability, are more likely to experience physical and sexual assault than any other women. Today, a female has more chance of being abused, assaulted, raped or even killed in her home by a male partner than anywhere else or by anyone else. As a consequence of these insidious patterns of behaviour, violence against women costs the Australian economy $13.6 billion every year.

Inevitably, since government agencies have become involved with Elsie, the day-to-day running of the refuge has become more corporatised, which is somewhat necessary given that 300 or so desperate families come through the refuge annually. Residents are now called 'clients'; applying for funding is now 'procurement'; 25 per cent of a client's Centrelink payments are tithed for running costs; and there is a time limit of three months on a client's stay. Workers no longer sleep overnight at the refuge and instead take turns to be 'on call'. Instead of being automatically eligible for emergency accommodation from Public Housing, as my mother and I once were, the clients now must choose between ever-changing federal programs.

When I wonder aloud whether my mother, baby brother and I could have survived on our own under such draconian regulations, Tanya, the manager, reminds me that today, the general waiting list for Public Housing is twelve to fifteen years, while the so-called priority list stands at two to five years.

'And what constitutes a priority these days?'

'People with AIDS and HIV', she replies. 'The elderly and those with a terminal illness or a disability'.

'Not traumatised and abused women and children?'

Tanya sighs and shakes her head. 'Sadly, no. Not unless they're disabled, terminally ill, or have substance abuse problems'.

***

It's been a long day revisiting the refuge, and by now I'm feeling traumatised myself, but as I prepare to leave, I pause to ask Marie and her daughters if they have any future plans. Given the difficulty of securing emergency housing, I expect them to be equivocal, but Marie is surprisingly resolved: 'The three of us are changing our names and identities and in two weeks we're moving interstate'.

'Like the witness protection program?' I ask.

She nods.

'Do you know anyone in the place where you're heading?'

'We don't know a soul', replies Marie. 'And we don't care. We just want to get as far away as possible from him!'

After I wish them well and hug them goodbye, I walk down the front path and onto the street, recalling again the years of abuse at the hands of my stepfather and how, as a consequence, my mother tried to commit suicide three times, the last attempt of which landed her unconscious and in intensive care for three days. Fortunately, she recovered and would soon read a feature article in the *Women's Weekly* about the existence of a women's shelter called Elsie in Sydney's inner west. Only a few nights later, after my stepfather went on yet another violent tirade, she grabbed my brother and me and dragged us, still wearing pyjamas, out into a thunderstorm and down an empty street, where she hailed a cab, shoved us in, and told the driver to step on it. An hour later we were sitting in the living room of Elsie, sipping tea and weeping with relief.

As I take one last look at the terrace, I catch myself thinking that if it weren't for the actions of Summers, Beaton and the others back in 1974, I'm not sure I'd be alive today. I'm also struck by the coincidence that now, all these years later, I myself am writing a magazine article about Elsie – and that there's a possibility that some abused mother or child will happen to read these words, pick up the phone, and find the courage to make that life-changing call.

LOVE

Love and Death in Darlinghurst

(2005)

When we began to fall in love, he was still living with his wife. The process was so gradual it was almost imperceptible, like watching ice melt. I didn't have much time to contemplate what was unfolding between us: my father was sleeping in my bed every night, while I lay on the floor in the next room, listening to his faltering breath, the short sharp wheezing after he spat blood into a bucket.

Louis and I met shortly before my father's diagnosis. A friend, writer Linda Jaivin, threw a dinner party and the other two invited guests pulled out at the last moment. A phone call later and Louis arrived to fill out the numbers, all long limbs and wild black curly hair as he bounded through the door. He didn't seem so much a man, but a force of nature, a whirlwind of stories, one-liners and witticisms that were seemingly inexhaustible. Over pita bread and red wine we chatted about the area in which we both lived – Kings Cross – and about how so many of Australia's most prominent writers had either lived in the Cross and/or had written about it. By the time Linda had served the entree, the three of us had decided to edit an anthology about the Cross. Of course, like most people, I'd participated in many a boozy, potentially great collaborative idea before, and assumed that the excitement of this prospective project would soon fade the next morning, along with our hangovers.

The next morning Louis faxed me to arrange a meeting. By the time the three of us convened at Moran's restaurant to sketch out a structure for the book, Linda confessed she had to drop out of the project, due to pressing deadlines. I felt conflicted myself. Apart from working on a screenplay, a short story collection, and trying to finish my Doctorate, my father had just been diagnosed with lung cancer and had been given six months to live. I would be his only carer.

I had turned up to the meeting prepared to bow out of the project, too. But Linda made her announcement first, and when I expressed doubts about the availability of my own time, Louis flashed me a look of such profound disappointment that I qualified my excuses and simply warned him that, during the editing process, my energies would be stretched.

We drew up a reading list and parted ways. My time over the following months was divided between measuring morphine, counting tablets, reading works by Kenneth Slessor and Sumner Locke Elliott, revising my story collection, daily walks with my father to St Vincent's Hospital for his radiotherapy treatment, organising blood transfusions, researching the history of Kings Cross, and struggling, with great difficulty, to keep my nerve. Louis and I would meet about once a week at Moran's, to exchange material and to discuss and shape what was becoming our man- uscript. I soon found, however, that he was a speed-reader and I could not keep up with the pace at which he devoured entire books. I, on the other hand, am slow and careful, re-reading paragraphs, making notes in the margin. I felt guilty about not being able to keep up with him. At one point, after I'd taken my father into the Emergency Department of St Vincent's, and had been informed that the cancer had spread to his lymph nodes, I faxed Louis and explained, with great regret, that I could no longer cope and had to pull out of the project altogether. Perhaps he could find a replace- ment, or continue with the editing on his own?

He called me immediately: he understood the pressure I was under, but wanted me to remain attached to the anthology. He would do most of the initial reading, and I would eventually vet his short list. *Just turn up to Moran's, have a glass of wine, and give me your opinions!* he said, with his usual jollity. This seemed simple enough, but I still felt uneasy about not being able to make an equal contribution.

Sometimes I'd turn up tense as a stretched piano string, faltering and out of tune to the subject at hand. The cancer had travelled up to my father's frontal lobe, which stimulated aggressive behaviour, and his usual warm and genial manner had calcified into a persistent vitriol: his food was never hot enough, his enemas weren't effective, all his doctors were idiots, and there was no way he was going to let a visiting palliative care nurse through the door to check his blood count and weight. It was the first time he'd ever yelled at me, and he continued to yell at me often. My greatest fear was that he would die, disappointed in, and withholding his love from, me.

Louis and I talked as much about these problems as we did the virtues of Kenneth Mackenzie's novel *The Refuge* and the deficits of Patrick White's overwritten prose. Anecdotes of incontinence dovetailed into a shared passion for Jon Rose's *At the Cross*, and these meetings slowly acquired the ambience of respite, throwing a small beam of light into my grief and diminishing stamina. The wine was a kind of medicine, and Louis made me laugh so much the knot in my stomach loosened. I guess it was inevitable that, over time, he would share some of his own problems with me. His marriage was in trouble, he confessed one afternoon; he was confused and didn't know what to do. Of course, I found this puzzling, but when I pressed him for details, he was evasive and changed the subject. I concluded that each relationship has its particular problems and secrets, and decided not to press him for a further explanation.

What I did enquire about was his childhood. Louis told me that his mother had murdered her own father shortly after World War II, and that he was born on the fifth anniversary of his grandfather's death, which was why his birthday was never celebrated at home. His father, high on speed, once aimed a shotgun at Louis and his sister and gave them ten seconds to run before he intended to shoot them both. Louis' gift for survival intrigued me deeply. Like me, he refused to be a victim, to be taken hostage by his violent past.

Back at home, my father's condition worsened: he grew thin and gaunt, refused to bathe, and barked at me relentlessly. He complained of a gnawing pain in his stomach, and after I took him to Emergency again for treatment he was admitted to St Vincent's Hospice.

It was during this period that I asked Louis if he would shoot some video footage of my father. Gerry was fading away, from the world, from his own life, and from me. I loved him deeply and needed to create a keepsake.

Gerry was wary of Louis at first, as he was of any man who might compete for his daughter's attention. But as the filming progressed, Louis slowly won him over with his humour and lack of guile. Gerry was impressed by Louis' snappy suits and snakeskin boots, and by his habit of always turning up to these sessions with a bottle of Seagram's Gin. By the third afternoon of shooting, we three were like a trio of old raconteurs, sipping martinis on the balcony of the hospice and trading stories with one another.

I'd put him to bed at eight o'clock, kiss him goodnight, and turn out the light. That was always the hardest time of my day, leaving him behind and closing the door, not knowing if he'd still be alive when I returned in the morning. Louis would walk me home, his slender arm wrapped around me, as if I were too young or confused to cross a busy city street on my own.

Gerry survived the first stroke. When he regained consciousness, after a twelve-hour coma, I realised his personality had changed yet again, and the sweet and genial man I had known all my life returned threefold. He was calm and affectionate. He began smoking cigars and his sense of humour ran riot. When the hospital barber entered his shared ward and asked if anyone needed a hair-cut, Gerry retorted, in his loudest voice, *I'll have a shampoo and a blowjob!* When he saw a fellow patient kissing the resident cat on the mouth – a patient whom he loathed – he declared with great glee, *Do you know that just five minutes ago that cat was licking its arse?* The doctor explained to me that the stroke had provided a minor lobotomy on his frontal lobe, essentially zapping out his aggressive behaviour. Sometimes, in the afternoons, he'd leave the hospice, wearing my purple satin pyjamas, and walk down the street to the Darlo Bar, where he'd sink a few schooners and hold court with the local bar flies.

He was released from the hospice between Christmas and New Year 1999, painfully thin, yet optimistic. He had so little weight on him that, as I was unlocking the door to my building, a blast of wind blew him over. During this time, Louis and I met more frequently, over lunch, sometimes dinner. The pretext was our anthology project, but it was hard not to notice that something had changed between us, even though, at the time, neither of us could have named it.

In spite of the fact he was dying, my father noticed this, too, and he surprised me by broaching the subject early one afternoon. *Why don't you two get together? You're bloody made for one another.*

I nodded briefly and sighed. *There's only one problem*, I replied. *He's married.*

This, however, did not deter my father, who had never lived by any sense of morality but his own. The last of our film sessions was in my apartment, early on New Year's Eve – a fresh bottle of gin, jazz on the stereo – only hours before the dawn of the new millennium. Whenever I left the room I could overhear my father prodding Louis: *Why haven't you made a pass at my daughter? You two are made for one another.* Each time he did this I flushed with embarrassment, but I couldn't help but admire him for his dogged effort to nudge us together.

Before Louis left that night, he walked into the bathroom, where I was washing my hands, took me in his arms and kissed me deeply, and I kissed him back, inhaling his delicious, earthy scent.

***

Ten days later, as I was handing my father his morning medication, his body stiffened, his eyes rolled back, and he fell into my arms, trembling violently, as if he were having an epileptic fit.

I rode with him in the ambulance, and after he was admitted to Emergency I was taken to a small room and was informed by a doctor that he'd had a second, more serious, stroke and could die at any time. I had him transferred to the hospice, where I knew he would receive the medication and care that would allow him to pass away as painlessly as possible.

I was supposed to have a meeting with Louis that afternoon and rang him in order to cancel. Within fifteen minutes, he was sitting by me at Gerry's bedside, pouring me a glass of wine and holding my hand. It was the most comfort and support I'd received from anyone – including my relatives. When Gerry regained consciousness, it was obvious even to him that he had very little time left. He'd lost his motor coordination and was now unable to feed himself or go to the bathroom, though he was able to hold a glass of wine in his trembling hands, to raise it to his mouth.

For a long time he held my free hand, repeatedly lifting it to his lips and kissing my fingers, my knuckles, over and over, like some dashing, medieval knight.

Yes, Gerry, I said, *there's not enough kissing in the world.*

No, he replied, glancing directly at Louis, and then at me, *there's not enough fucking in the world.*

It was the last lucid comment he would ever make.

Now, my father would always be unavailable to me, and the greatest distance of them all would forever circumscribe our relationship. Louis had videotaped part of Gerry's final hours, how he'd wheezed into an oxygen mask, the way he'd held my hand and gazed at me sorrowfully with glazed blue eyes. Hours later, after he fell into a coma, a nurse wheeled in a foldout bed for me so I could sleep beside him through the night. And Louis lay down with me for a long time, gathering me in his arms, stroking my hair. We kissed once or twice and then I passed out, exhausted by the twelve-hour vigil.

Louis was the last person to see my father alive. When he rose at midnight, Gerry seemed to be breathing and sleeping peacefully. An hour after Louis went home, however, my father finally and quietly slipped away, while I slept on, oblivious to his passing.

His funeral was six days later, on a glorious sunny day in late January. But before that, I had to organise the arrangements, inform family and friends, publish notices, and I did not have time or energy to meet with Louis and discuss what was unfolding between us. Even though my father had obviously given Louis and me an unconditional blessing, I felt conflicted about falling for an unavailable man, and, of course, I was grieving and needed time alone.

The service was wild and joyful, as had been my father's life. I organised a five-piece jazz band to play in the church, which was packed with musicians, actors, bar flies and relatives. After we carried the coffin out to the car, the band and congregation filed out and followed the hearse down Darlinghurst Road, which the police had closed off, all playing percussion instruments along with the saxophonist's fast blues. The hearse turned left into Liverpool Street and everyone repaired to the Darlo Bar for the wake. All this Louis filmed for me; these tapes would become a tender and moving memento of the last days of one important relationship for me and, though I hardly knew it then, the early ones of yet another.

He shadowed me during the wake like a chaperone, alert to any possible needs, buying me drinks, making sure I didn't lose my handbag. I found myself drawn to him like a plant straining for sunlight.

My mother was playing the bereaved widow, even though she and my father had been legally separated for over twenty-seven years and she now had an adult son fathered by another man. She howled against the chests of my father's old friends, some of whom she'd had affairs with decades before. When a fight between my brothers threatened to derail the evening, I invited friends back to my apartment and asked Louis if he could walk my tipsy mother home. He later told me she'd flirted with him in the lift, and, as he guided her towards my front door, she turned and leaned against him: *Don't get involved with Mandy*, she warned. *She's very promiscuous.* Inside, my sister collapsed in his arms, crying, while my irate younger brother was ready to thump Louis a couple of times for *taking advantage* of his sister.

After a couple of hours of this kind of hysteria, I murmured to Louis, *Let's get out of here.* We walked arm in arm through the main streets of Kings Cross, through pleats of neon and pulsing lights, and at that moment I felt completely alienated from my family and their behaviour. Few had offered to help us during Gerry's illness, yet now they were squabbling over his few possessions: his kit of drums, his CDs, his two pieces of jewellery. What perplexed me the most was that, during his last weeks, Gerry had worked so hard to ensure I would inherit some kind of happiness after his passing, yet it seemed my relatives were now trying to undermine his efforts. It propelled me away from them and even closer to Louis, who, with his arm tight around my waist, felt closer and more familiar to me than any one of my siblings or my mother. It wasn't that he felt like home; it was more intense than that: to me, the man already was home. Unfortunately, he had a home of his own, and it certainly wasn't where I lived.

That night he walked me back to my apartment and lay beside me in bed, his long arms around me as I pressed into his curly black chest hair. When I woke the next morning I was surprised to see him still there beside me, gazing out the window at the harbour. As I wiped the crust out of my eyes, he announced, very quietly, that he intended to separate from his wife. This, of course, was a surprise, given that we'd never had sex and, as far as I was concerned, weren't about to any time soon. But an even bigger surprise was imminent: he was going to discuss it with her today, that very morning, if possible.

I replied that the choice was his, but begged him to postpone the discussion; Gerry's death, the funeral, and the fallout with my family was more stress than I could manage in the space of a single week.

Louis merely replied, half-smiling, *I agree with your father — there's not enough fucking in the world.*

That afternoon he moved out of his apartment and into his Edgecliff office, where he would live for the next four weeks.

***

In early February, we took our first, short holiday together, at the sprawling Carrington Hotel, in the Blue Mountains. A room furnished with antiques opened onto a balcony, affording views of swirling mist and deep green valleys. Since the school holidays were now over, the hotel was virtually empty and, as we explored the winding staircases, the wide halls, the games room and library, we encountered no one. It was as if all the privacy and time we had yearned for over the months had been offered to us all at once, as if we were the owners of this vast, sumptuous palace and the bar waiter, the desk clerk, the chef, were merely part of our personal entourage. It was also a relief to be away from Sydney, and the speculative eyes of people not accustomed to seeing Louis and me arm in arm.

We were sweeping through the bar on our first afternoon when we finally ran into two other guests: I did a double-take and realised that not only did I know this couple, but the man, nicknamed Smedley, was an old family friend who'd played the bass at my father's funeral, only two weeks before. He and his wife, Tess, were staying at the hotel, celebrating their tenth wedding anniversary. They insisted that we join them for dinner that night in the Carrington's dining room, to help them celebrate. So much for anonymity.

Upstairs, Louis and I made love for the first time. Afterwards, he lay beside me in bed and read aloud from one of his favourite novels, Carson McCullers' *The Member of the Wedding*. It felt delicious to be snuggled in bed, listening to the cadences of his voice, the smell of his sweat on my skin. It was the first time in many months that I'd felt something close to joy.

Afterwards, we dressed and joined Tess and Smed in the grand dining room. The four of us were the only guests seated for dinner. A concert piano gleamed in one corner; chandeliers twinkled above; the hundred or so other tables sat beneath cloaks of white linen, all of which reinforced this sense that Louis and I were Lord and Lady of the Land. Within minutes, however, another couple – both of whom were in their late sixties – was seated in the middle of the room. We soon found out they, too, were celebrating a wedding anniversary – their fortieth – and had travelled from Canada to commemorate it at the same hotel in which they'd spent their honeymoon.

By the end of the second course, I'd invited them over to join us for a drink. A shy, grinning teenager, on his first day as a waiter, kept dropping plates and tubs of butter, and continued to return to our table with bottles of champagne for which he kept forgetting to bill us. A local woman appeared, as if from nowhere, sat at the piano and began playing Beethoven's Fifth Symphony with impeccable timing and tone. The Canadian man boasted that he'd sung to his new bride in this very room on their honeymoon, in February 1960, which was three years before I'd been born.

What was the song? I asked.

'*Some Enchanted Evening*'.

I whispered in the pianist's ear and soon had the Canadian up on his feet, crooning a rendition to his teary wife.

It felt oddly coincidental and yet somehow prophetic that this was my first real 'date' with Louis. Afterwards, I overheard Smedley remarking to the pianist, *Those two are celebrating their fortieth, me and Tess, our tenth, and these two*, he added, waving his hand at me and Louis, *these two are just starting out.*

***

I was renting an apartment in Kings Cross that was so small my writing desk was wedged into a corner of the only bedroom. It didn't occur to either of us that Louis could possibly move in with me. When the lease expired on his office he rented an apartment that was only a two-minute walk away from my flat, around the corner, in Kellett Street. He had no furniture or utensils – having left everything with his wife, and so I filled his kitchen with some of Gerry's old pots and crockery, his bar fridge, a mirror. It was strange to open the cupboards and see the shot glasses, the floral plates, the Irish coffee mugs that had been part of my father's home for over a decade, here in this strange, new environment. I also gave him one of my sofas and a large oriental coffee table. The only thing he had to buy was a foldout sofa bed, pillows and an eiderdown. I felt bad that he'd given up so much in order to end his marriage: a two-bedroom apartment with panoramic harbour views way out to the The Heads, his videos and CDs, his paintings and photographs, even his adored chihuahua, Ren. (A few months after separating from his wife Ren was hit by a car and killed.) Now Louis was living in a small, rented apartment on a block populated with brothels and a legalised heroin injecting room. But he didn't seem to mind at all; in fact, he seemed elated: *I don't care where I live, as long as I can write.*

The short distance that now existed between his home and mine worked well for us both in the beginning. Louis began cooking at night, either at my place or his, and we settled into a quiet, domestic routine. Having had a history of insomnia, however, I soon found I couldn't sleep well unless I was at home, and so we began spending most nights at my apartment in my high, queen-sized bed.

Now that we could enjoy more time together, we naturally began to introduce each other to our respective interests and hobbies. Louis, a natural athlete, tried to teach me how to play tennis, but even when I wore my glasses I could rarely hit the ball. He grew tired of waiting as I chased after it, or when I batted the racket against nothing but air as I continued to miss my own serve. After three attempted 'lessons' he never raised the subject of tennis again. Similarly, I was interested in learning swing and jive dancing and signed us both up for a ten-week course. Five minutes into the first lesson, however, I realised I'd made a mistake: Louis didn't know his left foot from his right, kept coming in on the wrong beat, and when he'd spin me around he'd invariably trip me over. I was relieved to leave the hall that night and, like the tennis lessons, we both silently agreed to drop the idea.

A great fan of football and cricket, Louis was appalled to discover that I had never attended a live sporting event, and further astonished that I didn't even know the difference between Rugby League and AFL. When he took me to a cricket test match between England and Australia, I made the cardinal sin of mistaking Brett Lee for Shane Warne. It was that day we realised how fortunate we were to be living separately: it soon became obvious to us both that I am a slob and Louis is anal retentive; Louis likes loud death metal; I prefer jazz; Louis has filled his apartment with chihuahua statues; mine is brimming with scores of vintage shoes and hats. He learned quickly that I dislike wearing perfume, jewellery and underwear, and adjusted his gift-buying accordingly. I soon learned that he refused to wear shorts, sandals, or t-shirts.

We continued working on our anthology, organising the material we'd selected into chapters representing every decade of the twentieth century. Sometimes, however, our professional and personal lives overlapped. One afternoon, I had the selection laid out in rows on the wooden floor of my living room and we were glancing over them, rearranging the sequence and discussing cuts for the final draft. Louis was making a comment about the dearth of Kings Cross literature set in the 1980s, when I found myself no longer listening to what he was saying. I pushed him down on the floor, on top of the rows of manuscript papers, wrapped my limbs around him, and put my mouth on his. His head was lying against an excerpt of George Johnston's *Clean Straw for Nothing*; my arm suddenly elbowed an extract of *Aunts Up the Cross*, by Robin Dalton. Soon we were rolling over Patrick White, Betty Roland and Kenneth Slessor, the sheets beneath us crumpling like dry leaves.

This irreverence brimmed over into our first overseas holiday. Any restraint we'd exercised earlier in our friendship was now completely vanquished. Six months after the Carrington weekend, Louis took me to Ubud, a town in the Balinese hills, where we rented a suite in a traditional resort for a week. As the days passed, the staff grew more and more perplexed because we so rarely left our room. At lunchtime, we'd order nasi goreng and cold beer through room service. When the meals arrived the waiter would suggest, politely at first, that he could organise half- or full-day tours for us: whitewater rafting, the monkey forest; wouldn't we like to see the silver mines? With each delivery, we'd firmly decline, until one day an exasperated waiter finally voiced the collective concern of the resort workers: *Why you no tour? Why you stay in room all day?*

Louis merely smiled and signed the meal docket. *We're on our honeymoon*, he explained, handing back the pen. The waiter glanced at me then back at Louis. We were both barefooted and wearing white cotton robes. An expression of relief, almost joy overcame him. He smiled, nodded, and backed out of the room. No one at the resort ever bothered us again.

We whiled away the rainy afternoons on our private verandah, overlooking a pond filled with goldfish and watersnakes. The marble bath was so big we could lie side by side in it. I was re-reading Marquez's *Love in the Time of Cholera*; Louis was devouring *Julius Caesar*. At night we'd roll around on the bed, amusing each other by making up limericks: I remember during one inspired moment I managed to rhyme *Charles Mingus* with *cunnilingus*. One day we were wrestling on the floor and Louis picked me up and threw me onto the four-poster bed, the drapes and posts of which suddenly collapsed on top of me, along with Louis, amid peels of raucous laughter. It did feel like a honeymoon, and when we returned to Sydney and our separate homes I felt a sense of loss. As I unpacked my clothes and sorted my shoes, I was surprised by how much I missed him.

After a year of shuffling back and forth between our two apartments, the unit directly above mine became vacant, and it seemed inevitable that Louis would move into it. The property had glorious views over Woolloomooloo and the Harbour Bridge, and, as we shifted in his furniture, we fantasised about buying both flats and installing a spiral staircase between them. Louis bought a four-poster, queen-sized bed and soon we could lie in during the mornings, gazing out the window at the peaked sails of the Opera House. Now, Louis could cook in his kitchen upstairs, bring the meals down on a tray, and serve them on my candle-lit verandah. If I were restless at night, trying to sleep in his bed, I could always slip down to mine without disturbing him, much to the delight of one of my neighbours.

Roger lived across the landing from my apartment. He was an overweight, English, unemployed accountant who had an alarming resemblance to Benny Hill. He occasionally brought home local hookers and had a serious gambling problem. He often left his front door open *to circulate fresh air*. He once confessed to me that he was thrilled to have Louis and me as neighbours. When I asked him why, his eyebrows did a brief, lascivious dance. *I love watching you both running up and down the stairs, half naked!*

Our anthology, *In the Gutter … Looking at the Stars*, was published in July 2000 and it was a surprise and a relief that in spite of death and divorce, the project that had united us initially had come to fruition. We toured Sydney, Melbourne and Canberra, promoting and reading from the book.

Of course, like most couples who choose not to cohabit, it was only when we were travelling – and hence briefly living together – that we learned the extent of each other's idiosyncrasies. I soon realised that my boyfriend, due to his violent childhood in a Public Housing estate, had a pathological dislike of Melbourne, so much so that, when we first spent two days there, the only words he uttered to me or anyone else in those forty-eight hours were during radio and television interviews. During a subsequent trip he refused to eat, became withdrawn, and confessed that he felt suicidal. Another holiday in Byron Bay brought on a panic attack after we bicycled through the rain, and I learned, very quickly, that Louis could not bear to get his hair wet, because, as a child, the sight of damp follicles caused his mother to go on a tirade.

Curiously, this odd behaviour drew me to him even more, as I knew that behind every mood swing and extended silence was a boy still suffering from a lack of love. *I've killed one man*, his mother often boasted during argument, *so I can kill another!* I learned that his father had mistreated him in another way, deserting the family when Louis was ten. When he told me a story about being a kid, sitting on the front steps of their house for hours, waiting for his father's promised return, I couldn't help but blink back tears.

In turn, Louis soon learned what brings on my own panic attacks and depressions, which are often triggered by noise: the groans of old air conditioners, the screech and rattle of street cars, the hum of a hotel room mini-bar fridge, certain pitches of voices, loudspeakers at railway stations. Having to listen to music I dislike isn't merely inconvenient: it's torture. My blood pressure rises, my stomach tightens and I break out in a sweat.

After we'd been together for about a year, we were invited as guests to the Adelaide Writers' Festival, where we were accommodated in a room on the second-top floor of a hotel. Unfortunately, the level above us was being renovated, and after we checked in all I could hear – and experience – was the din of jackhammers. That night I couldn't eat and didn't sleep. The following day I revisited the site of the women's refuge that my mother, baby brother and I had sheltered in for three months in 1976, when we'd been on the run from my violent stepfather. He had threatened to kill us many times, and going interstate and into hiding was the only way we'd been able to escape. The revisit ignited a panic attack, and when I fled back to the hotel room, the jackhammers were still pounding. Now, it was time for me to be suicidal. Louis later found me in the bath and sitting mute in the darkness. We'd already made plans to go out together that evening, but by then even he knew that he should not try to communicate with me. He simply closed the door and allowed me to grieve.

Even though we'd both been married before, it felt as if we were learning to let our guards down with another person for the first time in our lives.

***

His divorce papers were signed in December 2001, and he was left with less than a third of his former assets. Still, he seemed more optimistic and contented than ever, as if money and property were self-renewing entities that required little or no attention. Again, his grace and confidence impressed me: he went about his work each day with the same amount of intense concentration and happiness.

I always knew when he was writing well because there'd be no foot-steps above my head, no music, no whistling kettle – just the silence of someone ensconced in an imaginary world, the quietude of a man dreaming.

He proposed to me on my birthday: St Valentine's Day, 2002. Instead of popping the question with an engagement ring, he instead proffered a one-off black Armani dress and matching high-heeled Italian shoes, both of which fitted perfectly. The distance between us was gradually narrowing, both literally and figuratively, and the closeness we now enjoyed was almost visceral in its intensity.

One afternoon, Roger stopped me on the stairs and told me he had to sell his apartment *immediately* so he could move back to England and into the home of his ageing parents. I inspected the unit on my own initially, and found posters of topless biker chicks on the walls and, in the study, a list of Roger's most recent resolutions thumbtacked to a pin board: *lose 15 kilos, blood pressure down by a third; no more betting (except for the Spring Carnival and the Davis Cup); pay off Visa interest; no more women (except Irene on the weekends and Debbie when she comes up from Wollongong)*. It wasn't hard to intuit that Roger was in desperate financial straits, and that afternoon Louis and I offered him a ludicrously cheap price for the apartment, which a relieved Roger hastily accepted. The night before Roger was due to fly out of Sydney, he invited us to his farewell dinner in a local pub. There, beside him, was seated an attractive blonde 'masseuse', who was accompanying him on a weeklong holiday to the Cook Islands, before he flew on alone to London. To help finance this jaunt, he explained, we had to pay for our own plates of spaghetti.

Within a month Louis was living directly across the landing from me, only four footsteps away. Now, he didn't have to negotiate the stairs when serving dinner, or tiptoe around on his hardwood floors. He set about installing floor-to-ceiling bookshelves through-out the apartment to contain his voluminous library. Whenever we threw a party, the celebrations would start in his apartment and spill over into mine. Late one night he was in a mischievous mood and dared me to walk naked from one apartment to the other. His only disappointment was that no one else in the building was there to see me skipping across the landing.

Eventually, I collected my father's ashes from the Eastern Suburbs Memorial Park. Gerry had specified that he'd wanted to be cremated but had not told me what he wanted done with his remains. I thought about scattering them at Coogee Beach, where I'd swum with him as a child, or beneath his favourite tree in the Royal Botanic Gardens. Until I could make up my mind, I decided to store the ashes in an oriental urn. At the Crematorium, I passed the urn over to the clerk; she nodded and disappeared into another room. When she returned about ten minutes later, she had the urn in one hand and a rectangular cardboard box in the other. *Dad didn't quite fit into the urn*, she explained, *he was too big!* When I arrived home, I placed the urn on top of the box in an antique cabinet decorated with bevelled glass, along with the last bottle of gin we three had shared, only days before Gerry had died. There were several shots still left inside it.

Louis and I were married in St John's Anglican Church, on 2 February 2003, three years after my father's passing. Most of the relatives and friends who'd been sceptical of our union initially were there at the service, and my mother even refrained from making a second pass at my groom. The same band that had performed at my father's funeral played during the service. Instead of the 'Wedding March', the pianist played the old jazz standard 'Our Love is Here to Stay' on the century-old pipe organ while an old family friend walked me down the aisle. Instead of hymns, the singer Jeff Duff led the congregation in a rendition of Stevie Wonder's 'You Are the Sunshine of my Life' and Gershwin's ''S Wonderful'. I was amused to glance back and see everyone in my family on the left-hand side of the church belting out the lyrics, while Louis' relatives, sequestered on the right, stood in silent and embarrassed bemusement. After the vows were exchanged, the Reverend recited the Lord's Prayer and fluffed one of the lines: *Lead us into temptation ...*

Following the service, we *were* led into temptation, with Jeff Duff and the musicians as our leaders: Louis, the guests and I followed them, pied piper-like, out of the church and through the streets of Kings Cross, saxophones wailing, tambourines jingling, drums booming, even managing to pick up one or two street people along the way. We rounded corners, stopped traffic, and eventually marched into the Bayswater Brasserie for champagne, seafood and speeches.

My favourite moment of the celebrations was towards the end of the night, when I glanced up to see our tipsy Reverend on the dance floor as the band played Nine Inch Nails' 'Closer', his crucifix swinging wildly from a chain around his neck as the band hit the chorus 'I Want to Fuck You Like an Animal'. A fitting transition from the wedding to the honeymoon.

We spent a week on the coast of Western Australia, just a few miles from the wine-making district of Margaret River. I swam in the wild surf, Louis read, and some days we'd hire a taxi for the day to take us touring through the various wineries. Still, I managed to exasperate Louis that week by accidentally smashing several glasses and breaking the suite's wide-screen television set. *Thank god we don't live together*, he said, *I wouldn't have anything left!*

We divided our wedding gifts and returned to our respective apartments. Louis, the official cook, took all the kitchenware. Due to a drastic shortage I, the official klutz, claimed the several sets of glasses. Now that we were married, we contemplated briefly the idea of sharing the one home – a house, possibly, with a garden shed for a writing studio. But after one long, objective look of Louis' apartment, stuffed with chihuahua tea towels, mugs, statues and calendars; shelves of books on the porn star Christie Canyon, another set of shelves devoted to tomes on the history of mushrooms; his CD collection filled with the names of bands I could hardly pronounce, I wasn't sure it was a good idea. He, too, felt the same when he considered my swing music, the pink walls of my living room, my many hats and shoes, my fridge almost crawling with mouldy containers of food.

A year after we married, we purchased a larger apartment just around the corner from our building, a two-bedroom home where I could enjoy my own study and have enough room for a dining table and piano. Some friends and acquaintances thought it odd and possibly risky for a newly married couple to live apart. I knew what they were thinking: I was possibly giving my husband covert permission to enjoy a bit on the side. I would always tell the detractors that if a spouse wants to have an affair, living together won't prevent it. My first husband and I had cohabited for eleven years but that didn't stop him from fathering a child with another woman.

Louis now cooks dinner in my kitchen and mostly sleeps in my bed at night. He rises early and leaves before I awaken at around 10am, and we each enjoy a full day of silence to write uninterrupted. We often email messages to each other throughout our day, and it's pleasant to meet up in the evenings and go out on a date.

After I moved in to the new apartment, I bought a snare drum, similar to the one my father played. I opened the oriental urn and the cardboard box and tipped the grey and grainy ashes into the drum, filled the air hole with Spakfilla, then sealed up the skin. Whenever we have a dinner party now, we always end up around the piano singing old jazz tunes, while I or another guest plays the snare, and sometimes, as my husband refills my glass, he likes to imitate the nasally voice of his dead father-in-law: *There's not enough fucking in the world.*

My New Orleans

– after Hurricane Katrina
(2005)

At night I'd catch the Desire bus on Decatur Street at 8.30. It would circle the French Quarter, passing horses and buggies, the outdoor patio of Café Du Monde, the levee of the Mississippi, groan down Canal Street, and turn right. If I missed the bus I could run through the rough part of the Quarter and pick it up on North Rampart. It would then rumble down Royal Street, past Irish bars and squat, clapboard houses, to where my then boyfriend, as usual, stood waiting at the stop. He met me there every night because it was too dangerous to walk to his house on my own.

Yusef didn't live on Desire Street, popularised by Tennessee Williams' play *A Streetcar Named Desire*, but two blocks before it, on Piety Street. The difference between the two names was for me an amusing metaphor for New Orleans itself: it was a city of contradictions, extremes, polarities. It was a place where deep religiosity coexisted with hedonistic excess. Its citizens had the shortest life span in America. It boasted the longest social calendar, and yet had the highest crime rate of any major US city. In winter it rained for weeks and the bowl-shaped city flooded; in summer it grew so hot and humid people would drop dead walking to the local shop.

The reason I ended up in the Crescent City had everything to do with weather. My father and I had spent the summer of 1983 in

New York, earning a good living from performing an act on the streets, but by October it was snowing and we had to fly south to warmer weather. My father was a 63-year-old jazz drummer; I was a twenty-year-old tap dancer. It was my first trip overseas.

The first aspect of the city that struck me was the extraordinary quality of light: the sun seemed much closer to earth and its radiance reminded me of the sunshine of Sydney. The likeness was further enhanced when I glimpsed the old buildings of the French Quarter: the ornate iron lace framing wide balconies, the narrow streets, the squat wooden homes lined against one another made me feel as if I were in the inner-Sydney suburb of Balmain.

Once night fell, however, the city grew an aura that was uniquely its own. Bourbon Street rippled with neon light; strippers leered from casement windows; clowns twisted balloons into the shapes of boats and planes; magicians pulled doves from the sleeves of their jackets; jazz burst from the open doors of clubs; young black kids either shined the shoes of tourists or tap danced with bottle tops nailed to the soles of their sneakers.

One of their preferred ways of making money was to ask a tourist, *I betcha five bucks I can tell you where you got those shoes.* The stranger would usually try to avoid the bet, but the kids would follow and keep haranguing until the poor bugger gave in and pulled out a fiver. *I tell you where you got those shoes, man*, one of them would declare with glee. The kid would point towards the ground. *On your feet!*

My father and I moved into a claustrophobically small room behind a witchcraft shop on St Philip Street in the French Quarter. The room was sparsely furnished: one mattress on the floor and a wardrobe with no doors. The walls were a grubby and faded pink, and painted on one was a mural of a five-pointed star with a large, spooky eye in the middle of it. I later found out that the assistant warlock who worked in the shop, and who lived in a studio across the courtyard from us, had painted it himself when he'd lived in the room. Jim, an overweight man with a black beard and hair, and who chain-smoked menthol cigarettes, declared that he'd needed the mural when he'd wished to *walk through to the other side*. When I asked him where he went to on 'the other side', he dragged heavily on his filter and declared merrily, *Anywhere I like!*

All the rooms and studios faced on to the courtyard. Our other neighbours included a blonde stripper named Jo-Jo, who worked in Big Daddy's on Bourbon Street, and who whiled away her afternoons sunbathing in the nude. Up the rickety wooden stairs lived two gay waiters who often appeared in the courtyard at dusk, proffering a tray of vodka cocktails. Also up the stairs was a Vietnam War vet who used to bang on the door of the communal bathroom, screaming, convinced that the Viet Cong were just outside on the street and were about to ambush us all. And then there was Frenchy, a short, thin man with a southern accent who wore various coloured berets and who grew marijuana and other herbs in plastic containers. Frenchy made his living by riding his bicycle at night between strip clubs, taking dinner orders from the naked dancers and promptly delivering the requested meals for a nominal tip.

My father and I learned that these people were 'Quarter Rats', residents who lived in the French Quarter and who rarely ventured from it. In fact, one of the gay waiters used to joke that a Quarter Rat had to show his passport before he could cross the bordering Canal Street. I was soon to realise that much of the rest of the city was as equally xenophobic. In the paper I read about a 92-year-old woman who'd lived in the 10th Ward all her life and had never left it. The only time she'd experienced Mardi Gras and the famously decadent French Quarter – only two miles from her home – was when she watched it on TV.

In October 1983, the city was preparing for the World's Fair, which was to open the following year. Hence, street performers from the rest of the country were pouring into New Orleans, establishing themselves and their acts on particular corners (called 'pitches') and hoping to make a killing from the anticipated influx of tourists. The Quarter was in chaos, most roads were ripped up and full of potholes, sections were cordoned off, bulldozers sat mute at vital intersections and kids walked barefoot into wet cement. Fortunately, it was a tap dancer's paradise: on Bourbon Street every few yards lay a thick piece of plywood covering a pothole, so instead of dancing on the stone pavement, each night I could perform on one of those.

For our first gig, we set up halfway down the block from two corner jazz clubs. One was the Maison Bourbon: it had an all-white band and catered for white tourists. Across the road was Crazy Shirley's, which had an all-black band and a mixed-race audience. The doors and windows of both clubs were flung open, and the bands were obviously in direct competition with each other. It was easy to hear which group was superior, even though it had the smaller audience.

My father executed a drum roll and by the time we began our first routine we had a crowd of about thirty around us, including the midget doorman from the seafood restaurant across the road, the Italian magician I'd seen in Jackson Square, a clown smoking a cigarette, an elderly woman on rollerskates and, at my feet, about six or seven crouching black boys, fascinated by my footwork. Most of them were thin and shirtless, wearing oversized shoes. When I looked closer I could see taps hammered into the soles with large, mangled nails that poked out the sides of the upper like thin, crooked fingers.

When my father and I finished the first number and the applause erupted around us, one of the kids, sporting a black bowler hat, jumped to his feet and shouted, with great seriousness, *Who taught you to do dat? Shirley Temple?* I laughed, but it was only then that I realised that they'd never seen a woman tap dance before, let alone a white woman, and on the street, at that. He told me his name was Pee Wee and performed a shuffling step for me. *Hey, Pops!* joked another boy to my father. *What planet are you from? Where you got your spaceship parked?*

I told them we were from Australia, but they just looked at me blankly and no one seemed to know what or where Australia was. One of the older ones – about ten – assumed a knowing air, tossed his head, and remarked, *Man, you speak good English!*

By this time, the word had spread down Bourbon Street and even more boys were running towards us, desperate to check out the drumming and tap dancing white aliens. Two kids were almost dragging an elderly black man between them as they hurried him up the block. He was dressed in a Panama hat, an oversized, plaid, swallow-tailed coat and matching three-quarter-length trousers. And he was so short the kids' heads were almost level with the brim of his hat. They bustled him over to meet me and see me dance. *This here Pork Chop!* one of the kids announced. *He the best!* chimed the other. *He the best of all!* Up close I could see that Pork Chop had a grey goatee and must have been close to eighty. In a quiet, dignified voice, he explained to me that he used to tour the world with the famous basketball team the Harlem Globetrotters as their tiny, tap dancing mascot, performing their signature song, 'Sweet Georgia Brown'. Now, each night he danced with the live band in Crazy Shirley's, on a piece of plywood for tips. *See all these kids out here dancing?* he asked me, gesturing proudly to the boys crowded around us. *Well, I taught them. I taught them all.*

My father and I settled into a routine in which we worked on Bourbon Street six nights a week. In my breaks, I used to stand at an open window outside Crazy Shirley's and watch Pork Chop perform his whirling, intricate routines. I always felt sad and heavy whenever I saw him passing around his hat, a grand old hoofer almost reduced to begging. Pork Chop and the street kids mostly agreed that I was a good tapper – one night Pork Chop had even graced me with a compliment, *You dance beautifully* – but Pee Wee told me one night I didn't know shit about making money in New

Orleans. Unfortunately, it was true: my father and I had gone from $200 nights in New York to $15 nights in the French Quarter. Some of the reasons for this could not be changed: the southern tourists were much poorer and more wary of street performers, and there was an 8pm curfew on street performing on Bourbon Street (the nightclubs along the strip didn't want any competition for the tourist dollar).

Pee Wee picked up a deep flaw in my street performing technique. He'd seen the audiences hoot and clap during our show, and yet drift off down the block without throwing any money into our hat. *You can't be waiting for them to come up and chuck something in!* he cried. *You got to git out there and git it!* He began training me to be more assertive. As soon as I'd finished dancing I would swoop up the hat and pass it around before the audience had a chance to walk away. Collecting money in this way was illegal in New Orleans, but Pee Wee assured me that everyone did it and added that I would just have to keep my eyes peeled for the cops to avoid being charged.

Pee Wee did me a huge favour: our nightly earnings almost doubled and we could afford to buy luxury items, like vitamins and beer. He turned up to our pitch on Bourbon Street almost every night, to chat and watch me dance. In my breaks I sometimes taught him one of my steps and he, in turn, would teach me one of his. After a few evenings, I invited him to join me, and he flashed a gleaming smile, allowed me to take his hand, and we began striking out rhythms against the plywood board, my father playing back-beats behind us, to the dismay of the growing crowd. Even though I was twenty and Pee Wee looked no older than eight or nine, it soon became obvious that tourists and locals alike didn't approve of us performing together. White men would mutter to me, *Whaddya doin' dancin' with that little nigger. He's nothin' more than a little sonofabitch nigger.* At the same time, older black boys would curse out Pee Wee *for dancing with a dumb white bitch.*

But we simply ignored them.

The same tensions arose when, the following year, I began dating my boyfriend and future husband. We met by chance, six days after my twenty-second birthday, on Mardi Gras Day 1985, at a Brazilian wedding reception held in the famous jazz club, Snug Harbor. On the corner of Yusef's street was a rough Irish bar, and each day we were subjected to men leaning out the windows and shouting abuse as we walked past hand in hand. Another afternoon on Piety Street we passed a trio of black women, sitting on a fence, fanning themselves. Yusef was called *a goddamn traitor* and I was dubbed *a no-account fuckin' slut*. But the most embarrassing aspect of this racial divide was when other black men noticed us together on the street and would try to solicit me for sex, assuming I was a prostitute or just plain easy. The insularity of the city kept many old traditions alive – even the negative ones.

In 1985, Yusef and I married and moved to Indiana, but we returned to New Orleans many times in the next decade to visit relatives and friends. The first time I dropped back into the witch-craft shop, the owner informed me that Jim, the assistant warlock, was doing time in the Louisiana State Prison. He'd tried to smuggle an underage girl across the Texas state line and was arrested at the border. I wondered why he couldn't simply cast one of his spells, walk through a prison mirror, and escape.

The last time I saw Pee Wee was in 1987. He had sprouted into a teenager; his two front teeth were capped with gold, with a star cut into each, so the gleaming ivory of his teeth shone through. He now thought tap dancing was for sissies and had moved on to shining shoes. It almost broke my heart to see him so tough and edgy, especially when he took my hand and asked if he could come home with me.

The following year, I saw Pork Chop for the last time, too. Gaunt and painfully thin, he was dying of cancer and could no longer dance. Sitting on a chair on the corner of Bourbon and

St Peter's streets, he was selling autographed black-and-white photographs of himself in order to pay for his funeral.

In 2005, Hurricane Katrina swept it all away: the bottle-top tap shoes, the horses and buggies, the Desire bus and that 9th Ward Irish bar. The musicians have no instruments and voodoo queens have lost their mojo. And I can't help but wonder what happened to all those Quarter Rats, the street performers and shoeshine boys, the hustlers and magicians. Evacuated and scattered throughout the rest of the country, many former residents won't be able to afford to return. The US government can rebuild as much as they wish, but no amount of cement and steel can reconstruct the city's racial and cultural diversity, her boisterous, raffish charm.

Soon after the hurricane, a Creole fisherman caught an alligator in a flooded New Orleans bayou. When he cut open the stomach he found a human arm, still clutching a mangled cornet.

Sleepless in Samoa

(2015)

It was supposed to have been a romantic week in the tropics, all expenses paid. My then boyfriend, Louis, was researching Western Samoa for a screenplay he was about to write, commissioned by an Australian film producer. We hadn't been together long, about nine months, and were still swimming in the early waves of lust. I packed vintage pornography and a satin bag filled with expensive sex toys. By then, we'd already created a vow that would define our relationship: 'Everything is possible; nothing is forbidden.'

On the plane I was introduced to some of the more unusual aspects of Samoan culture: a native returning home was so morbidly obese, due to an unhealthy western diet, that he could not fit into the toilet cubicle. Two resigned attendants came to his rescue, holding blankets around him in the aisle while he dropped his trousers and aimed his piss through the open door and into the bowl. Beside us sat a perfectly coiffed female impersonator, replete with false eyelashes, heavy make-up, and bee-stung lips. Louis later explained to me that the person was a Fa'afafine, a boy who'd been raised from birth as a girl, not unusual in Polynesia, especially if a family has no daughters. Most of them made a living in Samoa by performing in cabarets.

We landed on the island of Upolu late at night. Through the open windows of the bus I glimpsed traditional thatched huts, bamboo pavilions and market gardens. The air was cool and scented with frangipani. No wonder Scottish author Robert Louis Stevenson had chosen to live and write here, I thought. The place was a fragrant paradise.

At the registration counter of the famous Aggie Grey's Hotel, we were the last to check in, and were assigned the final available *fale*, or traditional hut, in the complex. It was so far away from the main building, however, that we were unable to find it on a map, a piece of paper so riddled with circles and squiggly paths that it looked like an Aboriginal dot painting. After returning to Reception, perplexed and confused, we were assigned a teenage porter who led us on a ten-minute walk along labyrinthine tracks until we reached the chainlink fence that bordered the property. Here, at the end of the very last row of huts, was our very own *fale*, built in the shape of a hexagon and thatched with palm leaves. I didn't mind being so far away from the hotel's restaurants and swimming pools; the distance would be a bonus, I reasoned, and would furnish us with even more privacy and peace.

At dawn next morning I was awakened by a loud, industrial throb that sounded like a semi-trailer idling beside the hut. As I crawled out of bed I could sense the *fale* and the floorboards beneath my bare feet vibrating. Was it an earthquake? I wondered. I opened the door and stuck my head outside: in the light of day, and on the other side of the chainlink fence, I could see a rudimentary building made of corrugated iron and a sign that read, *Bottling Factory*.

Louis pulled on a pair of trousers and a shirt and went to complain at the front desk. Twenty minutes later, he returned red-faced and sweaty, telling me he'd been fobbed off by the staff, whose ability to speak and understand English had mysteriously escaped them. One attendant, however, had managed to explain, in halting pidgin, that the bottling plant only operated between 6am and 6pm every day, and so shouldn't interfere with our sleep at night. The relentless revving grew louder, combined with the occasional din of shattering glass. We showered, dressed and fled the *fale*.

After breakfast in one of the hotel pavilions, we took a stroll downtown, following the curve of Apia Harbour. Curiously, for such a hot climate, and in such glare-filled light, there were few awnings or trees to shade the streets. I'd forgotten to bring a hat but every store we entered had none in stock. And then I realised the obese man on the plane the night before had not been an anomaly: just about everywhere I looked I saw islanders so overweight some were hyperventilating and finding it difficult to walk.

We bought some local newspapers and retired by the pool back at Aggie Grey's. I read that the city was experiencing a feral dog problem, with mongrels roaming the streets and attacking pedestrians in packs. I also read that recently there'd been a series of unsolved murders on the island and local authorities believed the fatalities were linked. While I cooled off in the pool Louis made another complaint at Reception about the infernal noise filling our *fale*, again to no avail.

After dinner that night we decided to have a cocktail in the hotel bar. We hadn't drained our first martini glasses, however, before another two were promptly delivered to our table. I glanced up at the waiter, puzzled. 'Those men over there wanted to buy you a drink—' he nodded to three smiling young men a few tables across, obviously islanders, with broad, sinewy shoulders and necks as thick as palm trunks. We raised the glasses to them and nodded a thankyou, and they nodded back. Louis immediately told the waiter to deliver a set of cocktails back to them, whatever they were drinking. Minutes later, the men walked over with their drinks and joined us, shaking our hands and introducing themselves. Originally from Samoa, they were cousins who now lived in Sydney, but who'd travelled back to Apia to settle a land dispute. One man, Paul, was set to inherit his father's side of a particular mountain, a parcel of land that had been passed down in his family, from generation to generation, to the first-born male, for hundreds of years. The only problem was proving it to the western courts without the benefit of written deeds. Paul also told us that in Australia he lived in Frederick Street, Sydenham, and that he worked in the scaffolding business for a man called Tom Domican. Paul bought us another round of drinks and then insisted that we come and stay with his family and experience the true Samoan culture. His grandmother would cook for us and he'd take us to some secret beaches that weren't on tourist maps. He pressed his phone number, written on a coaster, into my hand and made me promise to call him the following day. Louis bundled me out of the bar and into the cool night air. 'Well, wasn't he nice?' I remarked, weaving tipsily along a path beneath flowering vines. 'I'd rather stay with his family than in that noisy hut'.

Louis linked his arm in mine and drew me closer to him. He explained that he, too, had once lived in Frederick Street, Sydenham, on the same side of the road as Tom Domican's boss, Neddy Smith, who was a notorious Sydney drug trafficker, thief and murderer. 'When Paul says he's into scaffolding with Tom, it doesn't mean he's in the construction business'. I paused and asked him what he meant. '*Scaffolding* is a euphemism. Paul's one of Neddy's standover guys and does his dirty work for him. We're not ringing him tomorrow. We're staying the fuck away from him'.

At dawn the next morning I was rudely awakened again by the industrial throb of the bottling plant. I thought of Paul's generous offer to stay with his family, but quickly dismissed it, particularly after a wave of nausea rose through me and I ran for the toilet to throw up. I felt my face flare with fever; sweat rolled down my temples and cheeks. I wiped my face and retched into the toilet again. My elbows and knees began to burn. Had someone slipped a mickey into my drink the night before or was my unexpected illness merely a coincidence? I groaned and staggered back to bed.

***

'Fuck this', said Louis, after he'd risen, showered and shaved. Since we'd arrived, he'd complained about the bottling plant noise several times, but the staff at Reception had continued to pretend that they did not understand him. He swept out the door and returned twenty minutes later with two porters, who proceeded to collect our luggage and convey it along the winding paths and narrow lanes, with Louis and me following, until we came to the main building of the hotel complex. We trailed the porters up a flight of stairs and onto the second floor. One unlocked a door and we were ushered in to a huge suite with floor-to-ceiling windows. There were separate living and dining areas, a kitchen, bedroom, modern bathroom and, most importantly, air conditioning. A wide terrace ran the length of the apartment, affording stunning views of Apia Harbour. 'This best room in hotel', assured one of the porters. 'This best room on island'. Before they left, Louis palmed them each a tip.

By this time I was so dizzy and disoriented I staggered into the bedroom and sat on a sofa. Louis sat beside me and rested a hand on my forehead.

'How the hell did you manage this?' I asked, gesturing vaguely around the apartment. 'A bribe?'

Louis grinned. 'I told them I was writing a travel article for the *Sydney Morning Herald* about Samoa and their hotel. Suddenly, for some reason, they could understand my English perfectly'.

The cool air and silence were a blessed relief. Louis returned to the living room and I decided to take a nap. I pulled the bag of sex toys from my case, popped them into a bedside drawer, and collapsed onto the queen-sized four-poster. There would be no lovemaking today or tonight, or even the following morning. I was still racked with nausea and my joints were on fire.

***

The next four days passed in a spiral of sweating, spewing and shitting. I was unable to eat and so began subsisting on martinis and Panadol. The only reception I could find on the TV was a cable channel that showed one movie repeatedly on a loop. It was called *Pay It Forward*, about the karmic fortune gained by committing good deeds to virtual strangers. I continued to read the local papers daily, following updates on the feral dog epidemic, and the recent spate of unexplained murders. A wife and mother of two had been discovered the day before, stabbed to death on her kitchen floor. The woman had had no known enemies and the police, perplexed, could find no cause. A concerned neighbour, however, had seen a blonde-haired woman running from the crime scene and escaping on a child's bicycle.

Louis spent most of his time in the living room, researching Samoan history. The screenplay he was writing was an adaptation of Robert Louis Stevenson's novella, *The Beach of Falesá*, which Stevenson had written in his home, only a few miles away. The story was about a European man who gets conned into marrying a local girl who secretly is cursed. Louis, too, read the papers each day and discovered an advertisement for a cabaret show, featuring the local Fa'afafine exotic beauties, at one of the nearby hotels. We hadn't experienced any Samoan culture since we'd arrived five days before and so that night I forced myself from bed, showered and dressed, and accompanied him to the event.

The show was to take place inside a long pavilion with a stage at one end. We sat at a bamboo table at the front and ordered martinis. Curtain Up was advertised for 8pm sharp, but by 9:05 the black velvet drapes remained unparted. After ordering our third cocktail we heard some yelling from the back of the pavilion and presently a drag queen in her mid-forties, wearing fishnets and a sequinned miniskirt, came clacking in high heels down the aisle, calling to someone behind her to 'fuckin' hurry up!'

We turned to see a chubby white man in his late twenties,

wearing cargo pants and runners, struggling to carry all of her luggage and equipment: a 1950s beauty case, a cassette player, several garment bags trailing feather boas. They both ran up the stairs and disappeared backstage. Five minutes later, music began to swell through the pavilion and she appeared from behind the curtain and introduced herself as Fifi. She was wearing a red satin gown, her black beehive sitting like a turret on her head, and holding a microphone. But when she recognised the opening trumpets to Shirley Bassey's 'Big Spender', she lifted the mike and yelled backstage. 'Not that one, you stupid cunt! The other one! My opening!'

Suddenly, the song stopped. We heard a rattle backstage and the sound of glass breaking. She rested a hand on her hip and waited, rolling her eyes to the thatched ceiling. After a minute or so another song was broadcast, and she launched into lip-syncing 'Black Magic', by Ella Fitzgerald.

The chubby man returned from backstage and sat at the table next to ours with an older woman. Fifi dedicated most of her songs to 'my man in the front row', or to the woman next to him, whom she referred to as her mother-in-law. By this time, however, we were more interested in watching the boyfriend, who knew all the words to Fifi's songs and would mouth every lyric back to her. It was during the interval that Louis told me that he recognised the man. He'd been in the newspapers back home recently. Apparently, two years before, he'd been appointed by our government as a diplomat to Samoa, and had caused a scandal by having fallen in love with a Fa'afafine and requesting permission to marry her. Such arrangements are common in Samoa, but not in Australian Foreign Affairs. The man had been given an ultimatum: give up the Fa'afafine or resign from his position. He'd obviously made his choice, preferring to carry the bags of a demanding diva than a job for life in the diplomatic service. In some ways, I thought, the story sounded like a contemporary corollary to the screenplay Louis was attempting to adapt. When we arrived back at our hotel room, I threw up again, swallowed two Panadol, and flopped back onto the bed.

The following morning – our last – I was still nauseous and burning with fever. Louis and I sat up in bed, drinking tea and reading the local papers. There'd been two new developments in the series of murders: firstly, the American FBI had been called in to investigate the serial homicides; secondly, the murderer of the wife and mother who'd been stabbed two days before had been apprehended. The female suspect who'd been seen by a neighbour escaping the crime scene on a bicycle had turned out to be the woman's husband: he'd managed to disguise himself by donning his wife's kaftan and one of her blond wigs.

Louis had one landmark to visit in order to complete his research: the final home of Robert Louis Stevenson, a five-minute taxi ride from our hotel. Having been a fan of Stevenson for years, especially *Treasure Island* and *Dr Jekyll and Mr Hyde*, I insisted upon coming along, in spite of my vertigo.

It was late afternoon by the time the cab pulled up on a grassy rise. We climbed out into the sunshine to see a large white, two-storey home with wide verandahs, surrounded by palms and tropical flowers. I climbed the stairs to the main entrance unsteadily, with Louis' hand on the small of my back. A young Samoan woman, with an American accent, met us in the airy foyer to act as our private tour guide. Ceiling fans revolved in lazy circles. Louis pointed to framed photographs of Stevenson and dark-skinned local natives from the nineteenth century – all slim, healthy, with fine, sharp muscles skeining their shoulders and arms. 'That's what they used to look like', he remarked, 'before the Westerners got to them'. Louis added that Stevenson had been highly critical of the European officials appointed to rule the Samoans, and had bonded with the local natives well, adopting the name *Tusitala*, meaning 'storyteller' in Samoan.

Our tour guide was clearly bored with her job. She showed

us through the home that Stevenson had built for himself and his family, gesturing casually at paintings and ornaments. In a monotone she explained that the author's wife, Fanny, ten years his senior, had been married twice before and had been a widow with two children at the time of their marriage. Due to the author's failing health, he and his family, including his now-widowed mother, made several peripatetic journeys throughout the Pacific in search of a new home. It was thought the climate of Upolu would be efficacious. His decision to marry the older widower, however, and to settle in the tropics, would turn out to be a disaster. While he may have written such important works as *The Beach of Falesá*, *Catriona* and *The Ebb-Tide* on the island, the guide explained that Mrs Stevenson had a rapacious taste for the finer aspects of life, demanding expensive extensions to the house, furniture imported from Europe and all the best china and cutlery. As the guide explained Fanny's extravagant tastes I felt my stomach flip with nausea. 'He worked himself to death', concluded the guide. 'He couldn't keep up with all her demands'.

It's always disturbed me to hear stories of talented writers and artists who'd married the wrong partners, partners who cared little about the effort required to produce the work, but who were happy to exploit the results. Pausing in the open doorway of his study, gazing at his wooden writing desk, I felt bile beginning to rise in my throat.

'Where exactly did he die?' I managed to ask, leaning against the doorjamb.

The guide smiled and shook her head. 'Right on the spot where you're standing now. What a coincidence!'

We returned to the hotel to pack our bags. Even though Louis had secured a late checkout, when we walked into our suite we discovered four maids variously vacuuming, sponging the bathroom, sweeping the terrace and polishing the furniture. They didn't want to rush us, they explained, but they needed extra time to prepare the suite for some very important guests who were about to arrive. As the maids swarmed around us in a frenzy of cleaning, Louis and I threw our belongings into our suitcases. We ended up leaving the suite at the same time as the maids, who locked the door behind them. 'Hey?' I asked one of them, as she dropped the key in her pocket. 'Who are the very important guests taking over the suite?'

'You know about all the murder now on the island?' she asked. I told her that I did. 'The FBI, they coming from America. They stay in this suite for all the week'.

The shuttle to the airport wouldn't leave for another hour, so we stored our luggage at Reception and repaired to the bar for final drinks. We'd barely ordered our first round, however, when I heard a man's voice shout from one corner, 'Why the hell haven't you called me yet?!'

I turned around to see standover man Paul striding towards us. He was frowning, fists balled, as if he wanted to have a brawl with both of us right there in the bar. I felt myself paling and tried frantically to think of an excuse. 'I've been really sick', I blurted. 'For all of the week'.

'She's been ill', added Louis. 'Vomiting, fever, diarrhoea—'

Paul narrowed his eyes and looked me up and down. 'You've lost weight', he added. 'Are your joints aching?'

I nodded and leaned on the bar. 'They feel like they're being roasted over a fire'.

Paul nodded and bustled us back to a couch where four of his mates were sitting. They made space for us both and Paul made an announcement. 'These were the guys I was telling you about. They didn't ring because—' he pointed to me '—this one's got dengue fever'. The men all glanced at me, shook their heads, and groaned.

'What's dengue fever?' I asked, as Paul handed me a martini.

'It comes from a mosquito bite. Like malaria. But the strains on this island are strong enough to kill a man'.

Three hours later, as we were flying southwest over the Pacific,

Louis broke out in a sweat and developed a fever. His knees began to burn and he writhed in his seat like a man possessed. As I reached into my backpack to find some Panadol for him, the bag seemed curiously empty. I placed my hand on a familiar paperback novel, a spiral notebook, my toiletries. But something was missing, and as I pulled the Panadol from an interior pocket, I realised with horror what I'd left behind.

'The sex toys!' I said to Louis. 'I left them back at the suite. They're still inside the bedside drawer!'

I expected him to be angry, or at least frustrated, by such an obvious oversight. Clearly, in those early days of love, I didn't know him well.

He wiped the sweat from his brow and burst into laughter. 'Well, the FBI are going to have a good time tonight!'

A Writer in the Family

(2005)

When Charles Dickens' mother finished reading *Nicholas Nickleby*, she remarked to her son about the character of the matriarch (who happened to be based on herself): did he think anyone as silly as Catherine Nickleby could have existed? As an author who borrowed freely from characters in his family, Dickens got off lightly: his mother obviously didn't recognise herself in the book.

I occasionally feel sorry for the relatives of writers, including my own. Even though most authors protest and say they 'appropriate certain traits' and 'combine characters' (which is often true), we all know that the morphine-addicted mother in Eugene O'Neill's *Long Day's Journey Into Night* is based on the playwright's own mother and that Christina Stead's novel *The Man Who Loved Children* is basically a memoir with the names and locations changed. The first dramatic moments a budding writer experiences are usually in the context of their family: the first characters they know will be their parents and siblings. The first fight they hear will probably be at home.

Most writers are ruthless when it comes to appropriating material, and think nothing of using any experience from the past or present to help them complete their work. William Faulkner went so far as to say that the serious artist is completely amoral, in that they will 'borrow, beg, or steal from anybody and everybody to get the work done … If a writer has to rob his mother, he will not hesitate; the "Ode on a Grecian Urn" is worth any number of old ladies'. In an article, Kristin Williamson (wife of playwright David Williamson) complained that in *Travelling North* her husband painted unflattering portraits of herself and her sister. 'Now I don't tell him everything', says Williamson, 'in case he uses it'.

So if an author who borrows heavily from their family isn't as lucky as Charles Dickens, how do they do their work well and maintain a relationship with their relatives? American crime novelist Jim Thompson waited until his father was senile before re-creating him as the hapless financial failure who stumbles home every night stinking of 'whores and whiskey' in the 1939 story *The Drilling Contractor*. Graham Greene enlisted the help of his progressive mother, who read Greene's books aloud to her invalid husband, always omitting the passages that might offend him. Australian author Nikki Gemmell attempted to publish *The Bride Stripped Bare* anonymously, mostly, one suspects, so her partner wouldn't read the portrayal of the novel's cuckolded husband. Some authors, like memoirist Augusten Burroughs, simply change their own names, thus sparing relatives any potential embarrassment.

Occasionally, the fear of embarrassing a relative can tame a writer. Two years ago, at dinner, a writer friend of mine told me he couldn't write about sex until his mother died. Three months after our conversation, she conveniently passed away. Since then, however, my friend has not written one single erotic word.

Perhaps the best kind of family for a writer is one that is indifferent to their books. The mother of novelist Helen Barnes has never responded to any of her published work, '—not even the article I wrote about the day I tried to kill my stepfather'. Nora Barnacle, wife of the prolific James Joyce and model for some of his major female characters, refused to read any of his books, not because she feared she'd find herself in them, but because she thought they were boring. One wonders if Molly Bloom would have been as feckless and lusty had Joyce known his wife would one day be reading *Ulysses* (once it was published, she only read up to page 26). I myself come from a family more interested in reading the TV guide than any of my books; I had the added benefit of a father who was virtually illiterate.

Sometimes, however, familial indifference is not always a good thing: Peter Carey once remarked in an article that he was hurt by the fact his twelve-year-old son wasn't remotely interested in any of his books. When my ex-husband, Yusef Komunyakaa, won the Pulitzer Prize for Poetry in 1994 (being the first African-American man to have done so), he immediately rang his family in rural Louisiana to tell them the news: unfortunately, they'd never heard of the prize and thought it was a sporting trophy. After receiving a phone call from me, my teenage brother left a note on the fridge for my mother: *Yusef has won Paulette Surprise.*

But for the relatives of an author, indifference might well be the healthiest response to the writer's career and work. Alas, this idea never occurred to Charmian Clift, who was so tortured by the possible portrayal of her infidelities in her husband's forthcoming novel that she committed suicide before it was published. Since the publication of the memoir *Wild Life*, John Dale's unsparing examination of the mysterious circumstances surrounding the death of his grandfather, his only remaining aunt and uncle refuse to speak to him. They strongly disagree with Dale's 'version' of their own father.

Similarly, when David Stead first read *The Man Who Loved Children*, he was horrified by the character of the cruel, domineering father, so obviously based on himself and only disguised superficially. He was shocked that Christina Stead saw things 'in so black a light'. Fortunately, he never admitted to Christina that he'd read it – his response was relayed to his son, Gilbert – but it must have put a strain on an already difficult relationship.

Occasionally, the families of writers begin to fracture because they know the scribe is the one who will define the family mythology, who will ultimately have the final say. A few years ago an irate in-law wrote to me, 'Is it because you write all the books you feel you have exclusive ownership of everything, or do you just like to control everything and distribute it at your whim?' Of course, having two writers in a family can be volcanic (the rivalry between sisters AS Byatt and Margaret Drabble, for example, is legendary).

Last year my husband, also a writer, and I discussed the possibility of having a child (between us we have published four memoirs, as well as many novels).

'We can't have a baby together', he argued. 'It'll grow up and publish a scathing book about us!'

'Oh, no', I replied, smiling, 'we'll never teach it to write'.

For the Love of Dog

(2015)

COCO

In 2005, two years after we married, I gave my husband an ultimatum: I wanted either a baby or a puppy – and soon.

The following week he arrived home with a chihuahua so small she could sit on my palm. The runt of the litter, she had blonde fur, deep green-gold eyes, and weighed less than a kilogram. As a child I was never allowed to have a dog, because my father forbade it. Ironically, as an adult, I was unable to have a child, because my husband didn't want to become a father.

We named the chihuahua Coco and the three of us became inseparable: Louis and I took her to the theatre, to the pub, to parties and on holidays. I had a bespoke staircase built for her against our high bed so she could walk up the steps and sleep curled up in my arms at night.

Louis taught her a few tricks, and she first demonstrated one of them at an outdoor restaurant, when we looked around and discovered her on a table, between the plates of two diners, begging for them to share their Wiener Schnitzels.

She also loved performing in public, and could shut a crying child up by merely pirouetting on her hind legs, or the offering of a high-five. She interacted so well with humans that in 2012 she was cast as herself in the ABC drama series *The Straits*, playing the beloved pet of a crime family living in Far North Queensland.

The lead actor, Brian Cox, made a fuss of her on the last day of the shoot, gathering her into his arms and gazing into her eyes: 'For the past forty years I've worked with apes, bears, chimps and lots of other dogs. But you, Coco – you're the best!'

One day, when she was ten-and-a-half, Louis was checking her fur for ticks and felt a tiny lump in her left armpit. We assumed it was a cyst, or some kind of benign growth. But when the vet told us that Coco had cancer, and was not expected to survive, I could not contemplate life without her. Her health and personality had always been robust: as a puppy she loved to run off the leash through inner-city parks and lick the faces of comatose drunks to wake them up.

However, now that she was ill, warned the vet, her life would change dramatically. No more daily trips to the pub; no more running off-leash through the park; certainly no more film work. Coco's immune system was so compromised that she could easily contract an infection from another dog. I transformed a corner of the kitchen into a nurse's station, where I would store medication, halve tablets and prepare her nightly meals. I'd cared for my father when he was dying of cancer in 1999, and this process with Coco was just as heartbreaking – perhaps even more so, because I couldn't explain to her what was happening to her, why she was losing weight, vomiting and had so little energy.

The first part of her program was to have her spleen removed, because the cancer had spread from her lymph nodes and tests revealed that the organ was about to implode, which would have resulted in a painful death.

She came home from hospital even thinner, shaky on her legs, with six stitches bisecting her stomach. That night she lay in my arms, trembling, while I stroked her and talked to her in a quiet voice. She recognises the word 'beautiful' – because that is what

LOVE

admiring strangers often tell her. And I soon realised that also saying the phrase 'You're so beautiful, Coco', over and over again, would be the only way to calm her down.

Once she'd recovered from the surgery, the course of chemotherapy began, which entailed several hours a week at the vet, hooked up to an IV. Coco weighs only 3.5 kilos, so the vet had a challenging task in estimating the exact amount of toxic chemicals to pump into her system – enough to kill the cancer, without also killing Coco.

Even so, her prognosis was not good; there was no guarantee the chemo would work. If the statistics were correct, her chance of survival was only 15 per cent.

In the meantime, the locals around Kings Cross and Woolloomooloo noticed that she was no longer walking the streets, and when Louis would turn up at the pub without her, everyone would berate him.

The mantra would begin at 5pm and not stop until he left at seven: *Where's Coco? Where's Coco?* One man from Penrith had brought his girlfriend down to the pub specifically to meet her, while two sailors from Tasmania had heard about this performing chihuahua and, after docking at Garden Island, had made a beeline to the pub in the hope of an introduction.

Once word got out that she'd developed cancer, however, and was enduring rounds of chemotherapy, friends, acquaintances and absolute strangers rallied around us. One day I was standing in line at the supermarket when a woman I'd never met before tapped me on the shoulder and offered to cook Coco cancer-fighting meals that included blended sardines and broccoli. Another, the mother of a friend with HIV, assured me she was saying novenas every night, praying for Coco's recovery. An artist with a club foot pressed a whole organic chicken into Louis' hands so that 'Coco can keep her strength up'. Even the vet, a doctor more than accustomed to sick dogs, texted me at 9:45 one Friday night, while we were watching the footy, to check on her condition.

But the most surprising response was from yet another person we'd never met, a local drug dealer with facial tics who had serviced transgender prostitutes in the area for many years. One day, when Louis was walking down to the pub, the dealer rushed up and asked, 'Where's the dog?' Louis explained about Coco's illness and her ongoing treatment.

The dealer hung his head and shook it. 'Mate, that's terrible news, just terrible—'

Growing teary, he pressed a fist into his pocket and pulled something out. 'Now, mate, look. If there's anything I can do, anything at all—' he handed over a crumpled business card '—you just let me know, mate, and I'll be there'.

At home, Louis and I fell into a military-type regime: he would take Coco to the surgery in the mornings for either blood tests or chemo; I would pick her up in the afternoons. He would pay the astronomical vet bills, and, because Coco could no longer go out, I would stay at home, day and night, to keep her company.

I didn't think it was possible that she and I could grow any closer, but during that winter, we did. And as the weather grew colder, we'd snuggle under a blanket on the couch and comfort one another. She could always tell when I was about to start bawling because she'd sniff at the air and lick my cheek. And whenever *Bondi Vet* came on the TV, she'd sit up and watch, recognising the whimpers of other sick dogs.

The email came through on Christmas Eve. I am not a religious woman, and I don't celebrate the birth of Christ, but the timing was kind of spooky: 'Coco's blood test this week is VERY good. The cancer is in full remission. Success!'

For the first time in six months, Louis and I walked her down to her favourite place: the pub. She twirled through the door on her hind legs, beneath the Christmas lights, like a diva returning to the stage after a lengthy absence. All the locals began applauding.

A plate of steak and chips was delivered to a table for a guy sitting alone. But before he had a chance to pick up his fork, Coco had leapt onto his lap and was already begging for a bite.

***

BASIL

The puppy was the size of a cup and tied to a piece of string. The owner, a local street person, sat on a brick fence in Kings Cross, rolling a cigarette. In front of him, three large, feral dogs barked wildly, straining on their leashes.

The puppy, however, sat behind them, as silent as a figurine. His peaked, bat-like ears quivered and he began pissing himself. He had the chocolate brown colouring of a kelpie, but was clearly a chihuahua, like Coco, who was then six years old. I remember that day clearly because I hadn't slept the night before due to a vicious bout of insomnia.

'How old?' I asked, jumping back from the snapping jaws of the others.

'Ten weeks', the owner replied, pulling on the little one's string. I noticed the pup wasn't wearing a collar, just the piece of twine that was knotted around his neck. I'd already heard stories about junkies in the area repeatedly breeding chihuahuas in half-derelict units to trade with dealers for heroin.

'Would you like to sell him?' I asked, glancing hesitantly at Louis. We were on our way home after a Sunday lunch at an outdoor restaurant.

'We're not getting another dog—' warned Louis.

The man smiled and said he'd consider it.

'How much?'

He didn't hesitate. 'Two hundred dollars'. I noticed he had a strong European accent, like Bela Lugosi playing Count Dracula.

I tried to talk the price down, but Lugosi wouldn't budge. 'You don't know what I went through', he objected, 'to get this leeetle dog!'

He unhooked the piece of string from his finger, picked the pup up and passed him to me, while the bigger ones continued barking. Holding him in one hand, he felt as light as a bread roll. I noticed his downy fur was streaked with dirt and that half of his tail had either been bitten off, or crudely hacked away by an incompetent breeder.

'Has he been vaccinated?' I asked.

Lugosi shook his head.

'Has he ever seen a vet?'

Another shake of the head.

I looked into the pup's eyes: a glossy deep brown, with the right one pointing sideways.

'We're not getting another dog', repeated Louis. 'All that toilet training again—'

I passed the puppy back and asked Louis to take Coco home, where I'd meet him later.

After racing around the corner, I found the nearest ATM, withdrew the cash, and returned to where I'd left Lugosi.

As we made the trade – me passing over the bills, he handing me the pup – I stepped a little too closely to the pack and one of the dogs lunged forward and bit me on the thigh.

Once home, I lied and told Louis that my new acquisition was only temporary, that I was merely rescuing the poor creature from a short, unhappy life on the streets until he could be rehomed.

'He's your responsibility', he reminded me. 'You know you're going to have to take that dog to the vet tomorrow.'

I knew I'd be able to talk Louis around eventually – but more importantly, what about Coco? At the time, she'd enjoyed our undivided attention for a full six years, and had made it clear she did not like the company of other dogs.

Fortunately, that month, she happened to be in heat, and not only accepted the immature pup, but flopped on her back and allowed him to sniff around her bum.

Our regular vet was based in the posh Sydney suburb of Wool-lahra, where she serviced pedigree poodles and award-winning golden retrievers. When I placed the puppy on the examination table, she picked him up briefly, frowned, dropped him back on the table and reeled. It was only then that I noticed he was so skinny and undernourished that his spine pressed through his fur like a line of knuckles. The sorry state he was in made me love him even more.

After a short and reluctant examination, the vet informed me that the puppy weighed less than a kilo, had a congenital heart murmur, a lazy eye and fleas. 'If you were asking my advice about whether to adopt this puppy, I would say, "No". He's badly bred and has a lot of problems'.

Her assessment of my new best friend infuriated me, and I became even more determined to protect this tiny misfit that I'd found on the street. So, the bemused vet obediently vaccinated, wormed, and de-flead the pup, cleaned his ears, brushed his fur and checked his anal glands. Once she'd microchipped him, I knew the puppy and I would be together forever. Later, I bought a collar and an ID tag and had *Basil* inscribed on it, along with my number. There was something about him that reminded me of the escaped rat causing hilarious chaos in the final episode of *Fawlty Towers*.

At first, he didn't know how to accept affection. When Louis rose in the mornings, Basil would meekly half-crawl towards him, with his head down, cowering, as if he expected Louis to clap him across the head. As time passed, and Basil grew more confident, he began licking my hand whenever I stroked him. He grew steadily and put on weight and his knuckly spine disappeared. He learned how to wag his half-tail, and would do so whenever one of us walked into the room, the abbreviated digit waving like a furry little finger. Within months, he developed a love of clowning around with his toys, especially ping-pong balls, which he'd roll down the staircase and across the hardwood floor. Then he'd chase after one, clamp his teeth around the ball, run back up the stairs, and repeat the game. Sometimes he'd merely toss the ball into the air and catch it in his mouth. I bought him some squeaky toys and whenever we were listening to jazz, he'd jam along by repeatedly biting his rubber pig in time with the music.

For the first few months, Coco tolerated Basil, but would jostle him away at night to secure the best spot on the couch. It was only after a trip to Cairns – and a three-and-a-half-hour flight from Sydney, trapped in one small carriage in the hold – that they finally bonded. I don't know what went on between the two during the flight, but by the time we released them into the tropical sunshine they were inseparable, together chasing flies, running after balls and stalking warty cane toads.

Back in Sydney, at the pub, we noticed Basil preferred to sit on Louis' lap. At night, he chose to sleep snuggled against his legs.

Louis became intrigued with Basil, and began studying him with a writer's eye. Throughout his adult life, he'd always owned pedigree chihuahuas, like Coco, but Basil was clearly a cross with a foxy or possibly a miniature pinscher. He noted the white patches in Basil's fur: a heart-shaped one on his chest, and a star-shaped one around his bum. When Louis rose in the middle of the night to use the toilet, Basil would walk ahead of him down the hallway, and Louis noticed that all he could see of the puppy in the darkness was that glowing white star-shape, which would guide him around the corner and into the bathroom.

This image of the white patch, shining like a beacon in the night, inspired him to write his second young-adult novel, *Prince of Afghanistan*. Louis told me it would be about an eighteen-year-old Australian soldier, Mark, who is parachuted into a dangerous rescue mission in remote Afghanistan, along with his best mate, Casey, and Casey's military-trained dog, Prince. When the mission goes wrong and Casey is killed, Mark adopts Prince and they embark on a perilous journey through enemy territory.

When he finished the first draft of the novel he gave it to me to read. As I ran my eyes across the pages I was surprised to discover a story about a man who was forced to adopt a Doberman pinscher he did not want and considered a burden. But as they cross the desert, the man grows to like and rely on the dog as much as the dog likes and relies on him. Mark's dependence on the dog is highlighted when his only guide in the darkest of night is the star-shaped white patch on Prince's bum. By the time the story ends, after enduring the hell of war, man and dog are inseparable.

I flicked back to the beginning of the manuscript and read the dedication: *To Basil – A Miniature Prince*.

The Gift of Life

(2013)

My brother had been waiting for a kidney transplant for five years when I could no longer bear to watch his suffering. A former athlete and basketballer, Jason had been diagnosed with acute renal failure at the age of twenty-four, and initially had been given just six months to live. Dialysis treatment went on to keep him alive, but it was a cruel and brutal regime. He was hooked up to a machine at home every night, unable to travel, to go on a date, or to consume more than 500 millilitres of liquid a day.

During home dialysis he nearly died seven times. Due to mechanical malfunctions in the night, he'd suddenly wake to alarm signals blaring and bathed in his own blood. He was living alone in Public Housing in the inner Melbourne suburb of Carlton and not long before, our mother had died. The least I could do, given the horrendous time he was going through, was to offer him one of my kidneys.

The screening process was rigorous, not only to test my physical health, but also my psychological state. After weeks of evaluations, I was thrilled to discover that, even though we have different fathers, Jason and I share the same blood and tissue type, and I was approved as an excellent match. Appointments were made; plans were drawn; yet at the last minute something strange happened between us. Jason grew hostile towards me, accusing me of ulterior motives, and changed his mind.

'You're just running out of material', he shouted to me once. 'You just need a new subject for the next book you write!' He stormed out of my apartment, leaving me stunned. I didn't know how to react or what to do.

***

'The reason why the kidney transplant list is so long', says nephrologist Dr David Goodman, of St Vincent's Hospital, Melbourne, 'is because dialysis can keep patients alive indefinitely, while those diagnosed with heart, liver or pancreatic failure don't have any form of life support and many will die waiting for a donor'. We're sitting in his fourth-floor office overlooking leafy Victoria Parade; it's the same office in which I first offered to be a donor for Jason, and Goodman is the same doctor who initially interviewed me.

In 2013, there were about 1600 people on the donor waiting list in Australia, yet in 2010 there were only 13.8 donors per million people. The average waiting time for a kidney transplant is four years, and each year 20 per cent of those on the list die.

I ask Goodman about our national reluctance on the issue. Is it a misunderstanding about the risks of harvesting organs before a registered donor is legally dead? He throws his hands up in exasperation.

'A hospital's first duty is to you and saving your life. Organ donation is only considered after all efforts fail and when organs can no longer function without life support. Two independent senior doctors have to verify this'.

Eighty per cent of Australians are willing to donate their organs, but only 60 per cent of Australian families give their consent for organ and tissue donations to proceed. 'Obviously, the most important part of organ donation', says Goodman, 'apart from registering, is to discuss your intentions clearly with your loved ones before it's too late'.

I'm curious about who decides which kidneys are donated to whom, and joke about a clutch of squabbling surgeons at an airport terminal, all fighting over the one available organ. Goodman smiles and shakes his head.

'It's overseen by transplant physicians in each state, based on blood group, tissue type and waiting time. But it's finally decided by a computer algorithm', he admits, 'which is national, with only a few minor changes for each state'.

'But who gets priority?' I persist, remembering my brother's many years on dialysis.

'Children', he finally replies in a soft voice. 'Children and those patients with type 1 diabetes who need a kidney/pancreas transplant. They do badly on dialysis'.

***

The dialysis building at St Vincent's was once a pub frequented by 1920s gangster Squizzy Taylor; its rooms now play host, not to Melbourne's underworld, but to those suffering renal failure. In a private room I meet Leanne Azoulas, who was diagnosed with type 1 diabetes at the age of eleven and who is now awaiting a kidney/pancreas transplant.

She's lying on a bed, wrapped in blankets, as blood is pumped back and forth through plastic tubes into a whirring, blinking machine to her right. With her pale face, large eyes and twig-like arms, I assume she's a teenager.

'No', she says quietly. 'I'm actually thirty-four'.

Azoulas' health began to decline when she was in her teens. She worked as a model and an extra when she was well enough, but for the past four-and-a-half years she has had to live with her parents in suburban Sunbury and undergo dialysis treatment for four-and-a-half hours, three times a week.

I ask how her illness has affected her personal life. 'You don't even have time for friendships', she says, glancing at the machine as if it were an obnoxious boyfriend. 'On the days I'm not on dialysis, I'm too tired to see anyone'.

Azoulas tells me that she was added to the transplant list only this year – previously, with her weight plummeting to 40 kilograms, she was deemed too fragile for surgery. Her stomach still can't process food or water, and so, along with her dialysis treatment, she has an IV drip in her arm for the intake of fats and nutrients.

Along the way she has suffered many complications as a consequence of diabetes: peritonitis, cataracts, and teeth so badly infected they all had to be removed and replaced with dentures.

'Obviously, I can't have a live donor', she says. 'And the other problem is, I'm blood type B and only 10 per cent of the population matches my type'. She admits that about two years ago, she wanted to give up.

'I just hit a wall. I didn't want to go on'.

We look up to see a tall man wearing paint-blotched overalls sweeping into the room. This is Kevin Green, Victorian chairman of Transplant Australia, who had to wait on dialysis for eight years before receiving a deceased kidney donation in 2009.

As he sits down and joins us, I ask him if he was ever tempted during that time to participate in organ tourism. His eyes widen and he nods. 'After about five years on dialysis I'd almost had it and was tempted to go to China'.

What changed his mind? 'First of all, the fee was $25 000 upfront. It's only an option for the rich. And secondly, if your body rejects that organ you can never get back on the transplant list in Australia'.

A former footy player, tennis enthusiast and swimming instructor, Green was diagnosed with glomerulonephritis at the age of nineteen. Assuming he was young and invincible, he resisted dialysis and refused to be added to the transplant list for several years until his kidneys began to fail and he was forced to reconsider.

Even though he comes from a family of twelve brothers and

four sisters, not one of them matched. 'I was kid number thirteen', he announces cheerily, 'the one who got the bad luck'.

I mention my experience with my brother, how he found it difficult to accept my offer to be a donor. Green snorts and crosses his legs.

'I know exactly how he felt. My best friend offered to be one. He was in his twenties and his missus had just had a baby. There was no way I could agree to that'.

Green pauses and begins chatting with Azoulas. 'Can you still have a piddle?' he gently enquires.

In any other context the question would be considered intrusive, but Azoulas smiles readily. 'Yes, a little bit'.

'Here's something you never read in the papers', Green says, turning to me, 'how organ failure often destroys marriages as well'.

'Soon after I went on dialysis', he says, 'my wife left me and took my daughter. So not only was I dealing with failure on a physical level, I was also suffering deeply on an emotional level'.

Green estimates that it happens much more than one would imagine. 'Of all the people diagnosed with renal failure, I'd say about 65 per cent would be left by their partners or spouses'.

He must have noticed the look of shock on my face. 'Look, it's understandable', he says. 'The drugs you're on make you cranky. You can't really work. You're flat out looking after yourself, let alone a family. Sometimes it all just gets too hard'.

Twelve of his friends have died in the past decade while still on the lengthy waiting list. 'The thing to do is maintain your health, before and after the operation'.

Green represented Australia in the 2011 World Transplant Games held in Sweden, winning a gold medal for golf pairs and silver for singles. He hits a button on his mobile and up pops an image of two children, Thomas, seven, and Meg, six, both recipients of live liver transplants when they were only six and fourteen months old respectively. 'These two kids are the faces of future Transplant Games', he says, proudly.

He leans over and looks at Azoulas. 'And next year you're gonna join us in the Games, too. Even if you only play Scrabble!'

She laughs and promises to be there.

***

I ask Goodman about organ tourism: has he ever had dialysis patients disappear, only to reappear two weeks later with scars on their torsos?

'Multiple times', he says. 'About five years ago a whole cluster of them went off to China together and returned with transplanted kidneys. The donors were convicts about to be executed and the blood and tissue types had already been matched'. (In August 2013, China announced it would phase out its practice of harvesting the organs of executed inmates.)

'I have strong objections to organ tourism', Goodman says, adjusting his frameless glasses. 'The donors feel abused. There's no follow-up care in China, India, Pakistan or the Philippines. The patients only get five days' worth of medicine after the operation so they fly back to Australia and get a cab straight from the airport to the Emergency room'.

Current studies suggest that those who receive live transplants have a 21 per cent better survival rate after twenty years than people who receive organs from deceased donors. I mention again the stoush I had with Jason, and Goodman nods knowingly.

'Ten years ago I would have said there would be very few complications. But recently we've lost two live donors, one in Sydney and one in Melbourne. It can happen'.

He says that here in St Vincent's recently, a mother donated a kidney to her daughter who was in her early thirties.

'The daughter lived', he says, looking down at his hands, 'but the mother died. And you can imagine the grief it has caused that family'.

***

At the Prince of Wales Hospital in Sydney, between fourteen and twenty live kidney transplants are performed each year. Recuperation times for patients are fairly minimal, with donors usually discharged from hospital four days post-surgery, and recipients taking seven to ten days.

In the downstairs coffee shop I meet Kenn Armstrong, fifty-three, and Tony Rogers, forty-eight, who met and fell in love in 1993. In 1998, when Armstrong was diagnosed with type 2 diabetes and left-ventricular heart disease, Rogers immediately offered to be a kidney donor in the event that he ever needed one. For twelve years Armstrong was able to manage his condition with medication and check-ups. In 2010, however, he suffered a bout of pneumonia that triggered end-stage renal failure.

Armstrong, a health professional working in the field of psychiatry, was forced to quit his job in order to receive dialysis treatment. It was then that Rogers offered to be a donor once more.

'It just seemed like the natural thing to do, without question', he says, linking his arm in Armstrong's. 'Kenn and I were stunned about the closeness of the compatibility'.

The surgery was performed without complication and the only side effect Rogers has suffered has been an increase in the size of his remaining kidney, which now has a double workload. For Armstrong, the transplant has not only saved his life, but completely transformed it; in eighteen months he has lost more than 30 kilograms, is sleeping well, no longer takes insulin and, most importantly, is no longer chained to a dialysis machine. I ask the couple how the transplant has affected their relationship.

'Well, we're closer than ever', says Armstrong.

'And now I like coffee and ABBA!' adds a mock-offended Rogers, smiling.

'And now Tony can joke about the fact that he can be in two places at once!'

Both men throw their heads back and laugh, but when I ask Armstrong what it was like to receive such a gift from his partner, he stops short and suddenly bursts into tears. 'It was very hard', he confesses, hyperventilating. As he continues to weep, Rogers puts an arm around him and says in a soothing voice: 'For a long time he said, "No", but I just dug my heels in. I just kept talking about it with him until he finally relented and changed his mind'.

Now, both men are looking to return to full-time work after three years struggling to survive on disability and carer pensions.

***

In his first term as prime minister, Kevin Rudd, himself a beneficiary of organ donation when he underwent an aortic valve replacement operation in 1995, invested $151 million in reforms to establish a nationally co-ordinated approach to organ donation, which has seen the number of registered donors go up steadily each year.

'Unfortunately, at the same time', says Goodman, 'we've seen the live organ donor rates go down'. He offers a shrug. 'I don't know if we've caused, unintentionally, those rates to go down, that people are presuming that because deceased donations are rising they don't need to consider live donation'.

Also, part of the 2009 reform agenda was the establishment of the Australian Paired Kidney Exchange Program, a system that allows a willing live donor who isn't a blood/tissue match with their intended recipient to register in the program to provide an organ for a stranger who also has a willing, but unmatched, donor. So both families essentially 'swap organs', even if they've never met one another before.

'How do you make all parties keep to their commitments?' I ask Goodman. He grins and makes a tent with his hands. 'The transplants have to be conducted at exactly the same time, even if the donors and recipients are in different locations. We could be removing a kidney in Melbourne to pair with a recipient in Perth, while a donor in Brisbane has part of his liver removed to donate to a child in Sydney. That's four operations happening simultaneously in four different locations'.

Today, Australia relies on three different types of organ donation: live, deceased and paired, yet many countries have taken more radical steps to increase donation rates. In July, for example, Wales passed a law assuming that all adults consent to organ donation after death unless they've deliberately 'opted out' of the program. More than twenty-four countries now have some form of an 'opt out' scheme, including Singapore, Austria, Belgium and Spain.

I put it to Goodman that such a scheme could work in Australia, but he disagrees. 'It works in more homogenous cultures like Spain. They all have a similar lifestyle and one dominant religion. Here in Australia it's so culturally diverse that it would be difficult to enforce. Muslims don't like to donate or receive organs. Neither do Indigenous Australians and some parts of the Jewish community'.

In August 2013, for the first time in this country, someone donated a kidney to a child who was not a matching blood type. Fourteen-year-old Chelsea Bury received a kidney from her father, Nigel. For Chelsea to be able to accept her father's kidney, she had to undergo a procedure during which the plasma from her own blood was removed and replaced by plasma that didn't carry antibodies that would cause rejection. The successful operation has paved the way for hundreds more parent–child donations with incompatible blood types.

About a third of children who need transplants have a blood type incompatible with either of their parents and so, up until 2013, have had to wait for a cadaverous donation or enter into the Paired

Kidney Exchange Program (in 2013 there were only ten to fifteen people registered for the program).

There have also been life-saving developments in the treatment of diabetes in Australia; in one case, surgery was performed on a long-term diabetic, extracting platelets from a donated pancreas and transplanting them into the liver of the recipient. In July 2013, the Gillard government unveiled a two-year scheme that makes live donors of kidneys or partial livers eligible for six weeks' paid leave so they can recover from an operation without too much financial stress.

However, a transplant is not a cure for organ failure; it's merely part of the ongoing treatment. Generally, a recipient who has received a deceased kidney donation can expect the organ to function well for about ten years, after which time they will return to a form of dialysis and await yet another transplant. For the recipients of live donations the function is improved: about ten to fifteen years.

Part of the treatment is the daily consumption of a raft of anti-rejection drugs, including steroids, the side effects of which produce high cholesterol, reduced bone density and severe mood swings.

Before I leave Goodman's office I ask him about the future. He is unequivocal. 'We need improved anti-rejection medications and just more donated organs. It's that simple'.

***

After eight years spent on dialysis, my brother finally received that all-important call in February 2008, informing him that a compatible donor had been found. Initially, the surgery went well, but he suffered lengthy post-operative complications as his body struggled to accept the organ.

Four weeks later, he was still in hospital fighting for his life — and with his doctors, who wanted to remove the kidney in yet another operation because they believed the transplant had failed. Amid the fighting and confusion, however, a nurse noticed something was amiss with the drainage tube in his stomach. She pushed a valve and litres of liquid suddenly gushed from his body, saving his life and, ultimately, allowing him to retain the precious gift of his kidney.

A fortnight later he was released from hospital. Due to severe nerve damage, however, it took him a further six months to fully recover and to return to work.

The transplant has allowed Jason to do so many things in the past five years that many of us take for granted: to eat and drink whatever he wishes; to play sport; to travel overseas; to go out on a date. Curiously, since our misunderstanding about my offer to be his donor so many years ago, we've never really discussed it again. The issue has just been hanging over us, unacknowledged, like an unpleasant smell.

***

I'm in Melbourne for the night and invite Jason over to my hotel for a drink. These days he's a slim, bright-eyed, 37-year-old who loves cycling and snowboarding. He's also fallen in love. His girlfriend, Jo, is about to give birth to their first son. I greet him at the door and we throw our arms around one another. When I mention that it happens to be Father's Day, we burst into laughter at the coincidence.

Sitting on a balcony, overlooking Fitzroy Street in St Kilda, I remind him that we never got around to writing a thankyou letter to the family of his deceased donor.

'I think they'd like to know you're doing so well, that you're about to become a father. You know, only 10 per cent of recipients write thankyou letters to families'.

Jason sets his eyes on a passing tram and sighs, 'What do you say?' He's not a talkative man at the best of times, and I can tell that he's genuinely exasperated and lost for words.

I take a sip of beer and brace myself for what I'm about to ask him, but I can't say it in the first person; it's just too hard.

'So why did you find it so difficult to accept a kidney from your sister?'

He sighs once more and rests his feet on the balcony railing. Laughter floats up from the street below. 'It's a gift', he replies, softly.

I wait for him to elaborate, but he doesn't.

'You know, the reason I wanted to give you a kidney', I confess, 'is because I totally love you'.

'I know that', he replies, a note of impatience in his voice.

He shifts in his seat. A tram bell rings. He keeps his eyes fixed on the diners in a restaurant across the street. 'And the only reason I couldn't accept it', he replies, 'is because I totally love you'.

A breeze rises up from the beach and trees sway against the neon lights. After a few minutes, Jason crosses his legs and remarks, 'You know this thing you're writing for the magazine, well, maybe it could be a kind of thankyou letter'.

I rest my hand on his, where I can feel his pulse, as steady as a drum. 'That's a good idea', I reply. 'Maybe it can.'

Goodbye, Pork Pie Hat:
Fourteen Ways to Say Farewell

(2013)

He'd been dead twelve years, but he was still in my hands. The prints were faded, the edges frilled with light. The week before, I'd found my father's old camera in a kitchen cupboard, with a roll of film still inside. I'd dropped it off at a local store and an hour later had picked up the prints: in one photo he's sitting in a Sydney pub, a schooner of beer in one hand, cigarette in the other. He's wearing a t-shirt from New Orleans, printed with *Always for Pleasure* in gold, and staring directly at the lens with a wicked grin, as if he were about to tell me a dirty joke. I flicked through the other shots: Gerry in his late seventies, wearing cowboy boots, dancing in an unfamiliar park. Gerry practising drums in his one-room flat. Gerry with his eyes closed, sitting beside a sunflower, smoking a joint in a friend's backyard.

***

He was the first to go; my mother, five years later. While he did not go gently into that dark night, she went passively – even deliberately – once she could no longer walk up the stairs to her bedroom or shuffle to the front gate on her walking frame.

Her final message to me is still on the answering machine. I can tell by the curl in her voice that she's had a few drinks, but is not yet completely gone. Nothing special. Just the usual 'Hi, it's Mum here'. Maybe she didn't know she was about to die, or maybe she didn't care.

I later learned that, as she was being loaded into an ambulance, my younger brother squeezed her hand and said, 'I love you, Mum'.

He didn't know it at the time, but she was about to utter her last words. Not 'I love you, too', or 'Take care of yourself'.

She looked into his eyes and replied, 'I know'.

***

In July 1999, Gerry was given six months to live. The tumour in his left lung was bigger than a walnut. He wasn't disappointed, he was furious, stomping out of the doctor's surgery and yelling, to no one in particular, 'Fucking cigarettes!' He was by then almost eighty and had been smoking, on and off, since he'd been a teenager. The jazz drummer's life certainly hadn't helped: long nights, booze and drugs, skipping meals, a fag for breakfast.

I moved him in to my one-bedroom apartment in Kings Cross, into my queen-sized bed with harbour views, while I slept on the floor in the living room. I'd been divorced only sixteen months and was still recovering from a decade-long marriage.

By this time my father was coughing up blood every few minutes and spitting it into a plastic bucket. He'd escaped death many, many times before, having survived being born with a cleft lip and cleft palate, numerous operations, a near-fatal car crash at the age of forty-eight, a heart attack and triple bypass at sixty-eight and, at seventy, a deadly melanoma so close to his brain a laser surgeon had to be flown in from the US in order to remove it.

In spite of the doctor's diagnosis of terminal cancer, Gerry kept praying – literally – for a miracle, saying the rosary every morning after he'd taken his pills. He still had lots of things to do – starting a funk band, harvesting his three mature marijuana plants, learning to windsurf – and this dying business was slowing him down.

He'd grow cranky over the slightest inconvenience: being served tepid tea, the number of ads on TV, not being able to have a shit after breakfast. The only things that would restore his good cheer would be a blood transfusion and an enema – and in that order. He'd then sip a glass of red wine and brag about where he planned to tour his funk band the following year.

***

The hardest part is not the death itself, but when you're confronted with a museum of relics, a conservatory of junk that no one else could ever love. It usually happens after the funeral, after the mountains of paperwork are completed, after the flowers stop arriving and everyone's gone home.

On opening the front door of my mother's Public Housing home, the first thing I spotted was the yellow glass ashtray beside her lounge chair, filled with the butts of cigarettes, the ones that eventually killed her.

The paraphernalia dotting the top of a cabinet: dusty ceramic frogs; a Chinese doll; a figurine of a shoeless boy sitting on a stump, fishing; eggs painted with miniature landscapes mounted inside plastic cubes. The curtains, once white, now smoked to the colour of drizzling rain. In the laundry, a pair of knickers soaking in a bucket of stagnant water.

A frilly doily of a bedroom: a nylon lace eiderdown and matching bedhead, a lampshade threaded with ribbons, a framed picture on the wall of a downcast kitten with Betty Boop eyes. Her wardrobe filled with elasticised trousers and cardigans bought from Vinnies.

Underneath the stairs: a shopping trolley, a walking frame, a walking stick that I gave her as a joke, with a retractable handle that held a secret whisky flask. The balls of used tissues beneath the cushion on her chair. A spice rack on the wall, not filled with oregano and thyme, but with Serepax, Atenolol, Valium, Nicardipine, Panamax and Mogadon. Under the kitchen sink, an enamel bowl with years of accumulated dripping inside, flecked with bacon bits.

It's a part of the process no one else ever witnesses, not the doctor, not the funeral director, not the priest, certainly not the close friends: the pilled sheets on the bed, the spare asthma puffer in the drawer, the set of false teeth floating in a cloudy glass of water on the crooked bathroom shelf.

As I looked at them I realised that one day somebody would be faced with my own gallery of private things, significant to no one but the person I'd once been. How would that somebody feel about finding a lock of blond hair in a ceramic pillbox? Or discovering a drawer full of defunct vibrators? Or the storage baskets under the sink in my bathroom, holding extra plastic shower curtain rings, loose emery boards, empty skin cream jars, tins of hardened shoe polish, a laminated student ID card from 1980 of a swollen-faced girl, wearing one earring, with circles under her eyes?

***

When my maternal grandmother died from a heart attack at the age of eighty-four, Mum was so bereft she sat on the couch for a week, drinking brandy and weeping – so much so that she was unable to fly from Melbourne to Sydney in order to attend the funeral. They'd been unusually close, especially after my mother's father had deserted the family when she was seven years old and run off to Tasmania with a woman he'd met at the General Post Office.

She'd lost her father early – and never quite recovered from it. Hence, my mother, who was the image of her handsome father, formed an unnaturally close bond with her own mother, Dolly, who favoured her over the other three children. And, like Dolly, my mother had spent most of her life chasing men who were either unavailable or incapable of unselfish love.

Only months before Mum died, I put an ad in the paper, in search of my lost grandfather or his relatives. I waited and waited, and so did she, but there was never a response. Even at the end of her life, she still yearned to be loved by the first man who'd deserted her seventy years before.

***

On my father's seventy-ninth birthday – which we both knew would be his last – I walked him through Darlinghurst to his usual radiotherapy session at St Vincent's Hospital. As he swept in to the clinic, he playfully announced to the staff and others in the waiting room, 'Now why is it called radiotherapy when there's no radio playing? How are we supposed to get better without any music?'

The nurses laughed and a woman hooked up to an oxygen machine chuckled to herself.

Later, back at home, he wasn't so irreverent. I'd invited a few friends around for a little party but a pain had begun to stab him in the stomach and he told me to cancel it. The pain grew worse; I put the bottles of wine back on top of the fridge. Half an hour later, he was doubled over.

I called his doctor, who faxed through a prescription for morphine. Desperate to make him comfortable for this one last birthday, I ran through Kings Cross, to the chemist across the road from the El Alamein Fountain, with the prescription in my hand. The bald pharmacist, who'd worked in the Cross for over thirty years, took one look at what had been prescribed and shook his head. 'We don't keep this stuff on the premises anymore. The junkies always hold us up and steal it'.

I tried the chemist further down, then the one near the railway station, and then the one across the road, where my friend, Hughie the drag queen, worked behind the counter. That night he was wearing a pink-and-white gingham '50s dress and a blonde wig. Hughie, too, smiled and shook his head. No one in the Cross keeps morphine these days.

I thought of my father lying on my couch, twisting in pain, unable to walk or eat. 'Please, Hughie', I begged. 'It's my dad's birthday'.

Hughie raised one long red fingernail to his lips and tapped them, as if punching data into a machine. 'Well, you could try Taylor Square. They're open twenty-four hours. Tell Bert that Hughie sent you'.

An hour later, I was back home, measuring the bitter-smelling syrup into a medicine cup. By this time Gerry had recovered slightly, having managed, in my absence, to open one of the red wines and fill a tumbler for us each. I handed him the cup and he downed the contents in one gulp. He paused, took a sip of wine, then grabbed the bottle of morphine from my hand and took another long swig, as if it were a chaser.

'I think it's working!' he announced, his eyes suddenly bright.

I sat opposite him, relieved, and kicked off my shoes.

'Why don't you have a hit?' he suggested, holding up the brown bottle. 'You look a bit uptight'.

'Nah, I'm all right'. I picked up my tumbler and raised it to him. 'Cheers', I said, and took a sip.

'No, go on!' he insisted.

I shook my head. 'I'm happy with the wine'.

He slid to the edge of his seat. 'You'll get a nice buzz', he added. 'C'mon, it's my birthday. Let's get high together!'

I looked at his sunken face, the pale, ice-blue eyes, and realised that, by this time next year, he'd be gone forever. The idea was preposterous – him not being around – as impossible as oxygen suddenly vanishing from the atmosphere. He proffered the brown bottle again and this time I accepted it. As I took the first gulp, I baulked: it tasted like lighter fluid.

But I kept drinking it down so I could also silence the sob rising in my throat.

***

The day my father lost his own mother he was rehearsing with his six-piece jazz band in the living room. By this time, in the early '60s, he'd been married twelve years and he and my mother had had two kids.

She was in the kitchen when the telegram arrived: *Mum died this morning. Love, Joan.*

Unfortunately, both my mother and father had sisters named Joan and she immediately burst into tears, presuming her own mother had died, rather than Gerry's. She banged on the living room door, summoning him. Then she noticed the postmark on the telegram – *Wollongong* – and realised it was Gerry's family who'd sent it.

My father opened the door and breezed into the kitchen. 'Yeah, Bet?' he asked. 'What's up?'

'This just arrived'. She handed him the message. 'Thank God it's your mother and not mine—'

The words were barely out of her mouth before she regretted them. But my father took no offence at all, just glanced at the telegram and shrugged. There were five men in the next room and they were in the middle of an important rehearsal. He handed the missive back to my mother. 'Oh, well', he admitted, 'she was old anyway'.

He turned and walked back towards his kit of drums, slamming the door behind him.

***

My mother deliberately smoked herself to death. She'd been warned, many times, that she would die if she continued but by the age of seventy-three she'd decided she'd had enough.

During one of our last telephone conversations, she was drunk, complaining that she was lonely, even though my stepbrother, at the age of thirty, still lived at home as her full-time carer.

Throughout my adult life, she'd pressured me to have children, particularly during the early, happy years of my first marriage, but by the time she was dying, all that had changed.

'Don't bother having kids', she exhorted. I could hear the clink of ice against glass as she took a sip of something – probably brandy. 'It's a waste of time. You spend your whole life looking after them and what do you get in return? A bloody card at Christmas!'

***

'Don't bother about a funeral for me', my mother always joked. 'When the time comes, just put me in a garbage bag and chuck me over the cemetery fence'.

When I miss her I like to wear her clothes – or, more precisely, her knee-length pink nighties. I flounce around my apartment in them, dancing to Benny Goodman.

And nearly a decade after her death, I still keep a tube of her lipstick, also pink, in my make-up bag. It looked better on her than it does on me, but every now and then I like to press it to my lips and taste her once again.

***

Cleaning out his one-room studio was more difficult than watching him die. He hadn't lived in it for many months, preferring either to stay with me, or to have some respite in St Vincent's Hospice.

By the time it came to sort out his stuff, clean the studio and return the keys to Public Housing, he'd been dead five weeks. Yet, walking into his flat, it seemed as if he'd just popped down to the pub to pick up a six-pack of beer or have a flutter on the races. A little like those scenes from Pompeii, with a single, inconsequential moment from daily life preserved in a lava of memory: the ashtray on the coffee table, knotted with roaches from his final joints; a racing guide with numbers scrawled in the margins; crockery and utensils on the sideboard, mostly stolen from pubs and clubs: glazed, white Irish coffee mugs, schooner glasses printed with AHA; a dinner plate from the City of Sydney RSL, another from Royal North Shore Hospital. On the wall hung last year's calendar, advertising his local chemist shop, with crosses and circles in certain squares, probably indicating his wins and losses at the racetrack. I opened the spare fridge and found piles of sheet music stacked inside, his treasured, private library. Under the sink, a bong made out of an Orchy bottle, still half-filled with loamy water.

The only thing of any worth he owned was his kit of drums, fully set up in the middle of the room, the skins and cymbals covered with blankets to keep the dust away.

In the wardrobe, not much, mostly clothes borrowed from other people and never returned: a couple of my old t-shirts and jumpers, one of my leather jackets, some trackie daks. A three-piece cream and tan suit that, for the past twenty-five years, he'd worn on special occasions. I could still smell his scent, like cooked oatmeal. I lifted the waistcoat and pressed it to my face, inhaling him one last time.

***

My mother's funeral was held in a Catholic Church, presided over by a priest named Father Fortunato, who clearly didn't enjoy his work. During the arrangements, two days prior, he'd enlisted my sister and me to read most of the prayers and lead every one of the hymns. At first, I thought his strategy was a compassionate one, insisting that the relatives of the deceased conduct the ceremony themselves to help them quell their grief.

But after the actual funeral began, I realised he was not only uninterested, he was clearly bored. He sat to the side of the pulpit, head bowed, occasionally glancing at his watch, and when he did speak briefly he mumbled so much no one could figure out if he were reciting 'Hail Mary' or 'Mary Had a Little Lamb'.

Towards the conclusion of the ceremony, when my sister went to sing a final song, 'God Bless the Child', he waved a hand, cut her off, and gestured to the coffin bearers to carry my mother away, which we did, lifting the casket to our shoulders and hurrying obediently down the aisle.

Later, outside the church, as people milled about, kissing and hugging, Father Fortunato emerged from the church, looking around, squinting against the glare. I watched him spot me and then make a beeline to where I was standing at the back of the hearse. He paused, hugged me, saying he was sorry for my loss. And then he admired the black lace dress I was wearing.

'What are you doing later?' he asked, stroking me on the cheek. 'I have some lovely red wine back in the rectory – if you like – to help you with your grief'.

✳✳✳

His funeral was on a warm, sunny day in the middle of summer. I organised a five-piece band to play in the church, which was packed with friends from various stages of his life. Whenever somebody stood up to tell a story about Gerry, they always apologised first to the Catholic priest, because Gerry obviously swore a lot and to imitate him truthfully one had to utter a lot of *fucks*.

Father Murphy, however, thought it was all hilarious good fun, and every time the band played a song, or someone told yet another funny story, I'd see him nick out to the side of the pulpit and guzzle on a goblet of wine, after which he'd reappear with an even darker red circle rimming his lips.

By this time, the singing had attracted the elderly nuns from the college next door, who stood at the back of the church, both mesmerised and shocked. Mesmerised, because listening to Jeff Duff crooning the song 'In Space, Everybody Jams with Miles' was pure and transcendental bliss; shocked, because the song defines the late jazz trumpeter Miles Davis as the one and only true God: *If you want to jam with John Coltrane, you've got to ask the man … You can hear them playing up in heaven, playing in Miles' Saintly All-Star Band …*

The nuns told me later that if a bishop had happened to turn up, poor old Father Murphy would have been disrobed and kicked out of the Church altogether for encouraging blasphemy.

After we carried the coffin out to the hearse, the band and congregation filed out and followed it down Darlinghurst Road – which the police had closed off – all playing percussion instruments to the saxophonist's fast blues. The hearse turned left into Liverpool Street and everyone repaired to the Darlo Bar for the wake.

***

'You've got to stop writing about your father so much', my mother admonished, again on the phone. 'It's like you're obsessed or something'.

I could tell by the higher pitch of her voice that she'd already drunk three or four beers. Tipsy enough to want to voice her opinions, yet sober enough to articulate them.

Two days before, my memoir *Dreamtime Alice* had been named the winner of the 2000 National Biography Award. The book was based on the three years Gerry and I had spent performing on the

159

streets together in the US – him drumming, me tap dancing – and even though the win was a pleasant surprise, it was also painful to realise that I wouldn't be able to share the experience with him. Bereft, I wore his three-piece suit and tie to the award ceremony at the State Library of New South Wales and of course mentioned him in my acceptance speech. The following day, a half-page picture of me in his suit, and quotes from my speech, ended up on page 3 of the Saturday papers.

'Every interview you give', my mother continued. 'Every newspaper article. You can't stop talking about your father. It's ridiculous!'

I could hear her dragging heavily on a cigarette and pictured her blowing it out the side of her mouth.

'He's only been dead for eight weeks', I replied. 'For fuck's sake, Mum, give me a break'.

***

One day, long before he got sick, we were sitting on my verandah, overlooking Kings Cross. We were listening to a recording of the jazz musician Charles Mingus, when my father asked me, 'Do you know the story behind this tune?'

I sipped my beer and listened. I recognised the melody but couldn't name the song – a slow, moody ballad with lots of backing horns.

Gerry didn't wait for me to answer. 'Well, one night in the late '50s, Mingus was onstage in a New York club, playing the piano, when a bloke crept up to him and whispered in his ear that Prez had died'.

I looked up quizzically, wondering who he was talking about.

'You know, Prez', prompted Gerry. 'Lester Young, the sax player. He always wore that funny hat'.

I recalled Young's breathtaking collaborations with Billie

Holiday, and nodded. I also remembered the funny hat Gerry had mentioned – a grey, floppy thing with a crooked brim.

'So Mingus', Gerry continued, 'he was a huge fan of Prez and so when he heard he'd just died, you know what he did?'

I gulped at my beer again and shook my head.

'Well, he was so upset he couldn't stop playing the piano. But instead of going on with the tune they were in the middle of, Mingus segued into a piece of music no one had heard before'.

Over my father's voice I listened to the trumpets and trombone soaring through the speakers, a shout and chant of longing.

Gerry drained his can and dropped it on the ground. 'You see, the tempo slowed right down and the rest of the band had to listen hard so that they could pick up the changes'. He slid to the edge of his chair, grinning. Sunlight angled through the leaves of a plane tree across the street and he closed his eyes against the glare.

'But what they didn't know', he added, 'was that Mingus was inventing the tune as he went along – he was improvising, you know – he was composing his farewell, moment by moment'.

Gerry's eyes suddenly snapped open and he leaned into a shadow. 'And you know what Mingus called the tune?'

I shook my head.

'He called it "Goodbye, Pork Pie Hat"'.

I glanced at my father, at his helmet of thick blond hair, his scarred lips and crooked nose, and wanted to remain sitting in the sun, in this moment with him, forever.

LITERATURE
AND ART

Thea Astley Comes Out
of the Shadows

(1996)

Since 1985, Thea Astley has lived with her husband, Jack Gregson, in the green dairy country of the NSW South Coast. In less than an hour, I shall be meeting the writer whose works I have admired so much. But as I'm sitting on the train, on my way to Nowra, I feel somewhat defeated: I've recently finished a draft of a book I've been working on for eleven years, but I know it still has weaknesses, and all I want to do is flee back home and tear the whole thing up.

I distract myself by contemplating Astley's paradoxical career: she has produced one of the most significant bodies of work for a female Australian novelist – fifteen books in all. Yet, thus far, not one full-length critical study of her work has been published. She has won many major literary awards, but the reviews of her novels have often been mixed. She has actively promoted her work at writers' festivals and in the media and yet hardly any of my friends have read her novels.

When the train pulls in to Nowra station, I recognise her immediately: the round and gentle face, so familiar from author photographs. She refuses to let me book in to a hotel, and instead bundles me into the car and insists I spend the night with her and Jack. 'We've got a spare room', she says, swinging the car on to the deserted main street.

I first began to read Astley in the late 1980s, when I was studying at Indiana University. Moored in the soya bean country of the American Midwest, I read her out of loneliness, out of longing for her tropical rainforests and dusty outback towns. I often found myself pushing away my assigned Shelley and Melville and sinking into the prose of Astley's *Hunting the Wild Pineapple* or *Reaching Tin River*. And suddenly I was no longer alone.

At the same time, I was beginning to write seriously myself, and keeping company with authors like Astley was both a comfort and an encouragement. Not only was she Australian, she was a woman – a kind of literary grandmother to whom I could turn when the looming precedents of the great American and English authors held little currency.

There were several qualities that distinguished her work for me: the poetic texture of her prose; the quirky, anecdotal humour; the unabashed feminism. There were things to be learned from reading Astley. I realised very early on, for example, that one of her favourite technical strategies was to set her novels in tiny outback towns, or on small islands or boats, thereby creating a microcosm of the world. It was she who illustrated what several of my teachers were trying to convey: that you achieve the universal through the particular. This realisation was developed when I read a famous Astley quote: 'Literary truth is derived from the parish, and if it is truth then it will be universal.'

It's a quote that is still stuck above my desk, and continues to exert an influence: During the writing of my most recent book, *The Cross*, I was trying quite deliberately to engage with large, timeless themes through the creation of a microcosm. I wanted to explore issues like our human need for continuity amid the inevitability of change by setting the novel on one Sydney street in 1975.

***

Astley and her husband live in a five-bedroom house on just over two hectares. Their spacious, sunny home is solar-powered, and a wood-burning stove keeps the place toasty. I've come to try and understand a little more about the force behind a 71-year-old woman who has continued to write and publish a book every two or three years since 1958, five years before I was born.

Sipping tea after lunch, she begins the story of her life. Born in Brisbane in 1925, Astley originally began to write poetry, but in her twenties switched to prose. At seventeen, she completed her Leaving Certificate and began teaching in the Queensland public school system the following year. Nights were spent working on a university degree: at the end of each week, she either rode in the back of a worker's truck or caught a steam train into Brisbane for evening lectures.

After four years of external study, she was awarded her arts degree in 1947 and was transferred to a school in Townsville. The only accommodation she could secure so soon after the war was a room that she shared with another woman who had a five-year-old child. Even then, Astley curled up on her single bed at night and wrote poetry and essays.

Following a string of positions in outback Queensland schools, she married Jack Gregson, whom she met at a Brisbane chamber music concert, and the couple moved to Sydney. Until 1980, Astley had a full-time position as a fellow in Australian literature at Macquarie University while raising their son, Ed, and continuing to write.

When I comment on her prolific output amid full-time work and caring for a family, Astley merely smiles. 'Well, Jack's been very supportive. And teaching's one of those jobs you can combine with parenthood because you can drive to school and drop the kids off, and the holidays coincide'.

I wonder who her antecedents were, who inspired her when she was starting out. 'Well, I didn't come to Christina Stead until later because she was ignored in this country. When [poet and critic] Randall Jarrell brought out an edition of *The Man Who Loved Children*, it knocked me sideways. But that wasn't until the late '60s. My dad was a journalist, and my maternal grandfather was a journalist. I always had the feeling that women's writing had no currency at all. I don't know what made me persist. Well, Ruth Park was writing. She's about my age'.

Recalling an incident at Macquarie University in 1970, she says, 'I was lecturing on [Henry Handel Richardson's] *The Fortunes of Richard Mahony*, and this young man came up to me afterwards and said, "Did you say that was written by a woman?" And I said, "Yes". And he said, "Well, I shan't read it then". And I said, "Well, in that case, I shall make it a compulsory question on the exam". And I did. And he didn't answer the question. And I failed him'.

Astley also recalls sending poems to the *Sydney Morning Herald* in 1956. When she submitted them under the pseudonym Phillip Cressy she was paid five guineas; when she submitted them under the name Thea Astley she was paid three guineas.

Over the years, I feel as if I've gained short bursts of enlightenment not only by reading Astley's work, but also by identifying with her experiences as an Australian woman writer. In the many interviews she has given throughout her career, Astley has made no bones about the fact that she grew up in a culture that believed women had no brains or opinions of their own. Of course, since the 1960s and '70s the expectations this country has of its young women have greatly increased, but as recently as 1989, when I won the Vogel Award for my first novel, the first question levelled at me during my first interview was not about some aspect of my book, but whether or not I was planning to have children.

When I mention this, Astley smiles. 'I remember being at a party once, very early on. I think I had one book out. And some man said to me in a condescending voice, "What do you write, Thea?

Love stories?" I said, "No, lust stories". And he vanished. I never saw him again'.

I love this defiant air about her. It's a kind of streamlined stubbornness that allows her to give as good as she gets. And it manifests itself in many ways: she refuses to give up smoking; she refuses to be photographed in profile; she refuses to let me help her load firewood into her wheelbarrow.

Astley admits that she had planned to retire from writing two years ago, after publishing the novel *Coda*. 'That's why I named it that', she says. 'I do think one ought to know when to stop'. However, a few years ago she read about a historical incident: a man living on a mission island off the Queensland coast went berserk with a rifle and a box of gelignite, shooting two of his staff members and blowing up his children as they slept in their beds. The article inspired her to do further research, and after one year of musing, and a further two years of writing, what has emerged is yet another accomplished novel.

The *Multiple Effects of Rainshadow* is a complex work, divided into chapters detailing the consequences of the tragedy for each main character inhabiting Astley's fictional island. It's yet another microcosm, headed by the crazed, obsessive Captain Brodie. One of the novel's features is the way in which Astley penetrates the erratic circuitry of a madman's mind to deliver an authentic account of the causes behind random violence.

One can't help but read this book in reference to the bloodshed at Port Arthur in April 1996, when Martin Bryant's shooting spree resulted in the murder of thirty-five innocent people. As the book's publisher claims: 'His [Captain Brodie's] violence is, in fact, a mirror for the brutality of Australian life.'

When I raise this issue with Astley, she becomes passionate: 'More and more, as I age, I find it intolerable that the laws and moral tenets of behaviour are administered by males when males commit 90 per cent of the crimes'. Later on, she is even more adamant: 'I've never been interested in politics until that marvellous man Gough Whitlam brought the troops back from Vietnam overnight. If he can do that overnight, I don't see why they can't get rid of guns overnight. When they had the troops coming back from Vietnam, it must've been the last time I had a small drink of radiant joy'.

***

Rainshadow's main female character, Mrs Curthoys, has a modest edict by which she lives: 'I always believe in coping', and it's not hard to sense that the phrase is also a projection of Astley's ethos. 'Well, the nuns always said to us, "Control yourself". And I was taught by nuns who lowered their voices. The softer they got, the more terrifying they were. But I'm glad I went to a convent school. They taught me self-control and self-discipline'.

Her early grounding in discipline has no doubt contributed to her ability to keep producing award-winning books that span almost four decades. Astley has won the Miles Franklin award three times (1962, 1965, 1972), the 1975 Australian Book of the Year, and the 1980 James Cook Award, among others.

Her career, however, has not all been gold medals and accolades. Astley is a writer who has not enjoyed the popular success of Thomas Keneally or the critical recognition of Patrick White. In an interview in 1989, she admitted her hardback print runs had barely transcended the 2000 to 3000 copies with which her career began.

Astley herself is not sure why, and shrugs off the figures, maintaining that she writes primarily for herself. Unlike Keneally, she has never positioned herself in the marketplace as a 'popular' writer. And I would venture to say that her books are an acquired taste — her prose is at once poetic, quirky and literary. She is not an 'easy read'.

Elizabeth Webby, professor of Australian literature at the University of Sydney, believes Astley has never achieved the attention she deserves because of the era in which she began publishing. 'Thea started writing at a pre-feminist time, in the '50s', Webby says. 'By the time public interest in women's writing increased in the '70s with writers like Elizabeth Jolley and Olga Masters, Astley had already been around for twenty years or so. People took her for granted. You can't be "discovered" after twenty years'.

Particularly in the early part of her career, Astley had to endure many negative reviews. Arthur Ashwood stated in a 1966 edition of *Southerly* that her second novel, *A Descant for Gossips*, failed because its technique was inadequate and the plot was contrived. In 1967, JM Cooper claimed in *Meanjin* that her first four novels were marred by unevenness. Two years later in the same journal, Laurie Clancy announced that she was 'an exasperating novelist'.

'Oh, some of them—' remarks Astley '—I've just been so hurt. Just gone away and howled'.

One gets the feeling, however, that it wasn't just that convent discipline that spurred her on in spite of the critics. It was that steely defiance again, coupled with her deep love of language.

Her flowering as a writer despite negative reviews is a quality she obviously shared with her friend and early mentor, Patrick White. Astley recalls her first response after reading *The Tree of Man*, which occurred before she'd been introduced to the famous man of Australian letters. 'I rushed outside and said to Jack, "My God! It's happened! It's started! At last, they're writing in this country". And AD Hope wrote this appalling review, because he wasn't used to poetic prose. Patrick told me the day that review came out; he walked down to get the paper at midday. I can still remember exactly what he said when he read it: "I felt sick"'.

Astley and White first met in the late 1950s, when they lived close to one another in Sydney's northern suburbs – Astley in Epping and White in Castle Hill. White provided encouragement to the blossoming writer, and was no doubt a source of inspiration. 'I thought he was awfully nice', muses Astley. 'He had a great streak of generosity as well. I'm not talking in financial terms, but about other people's work'.

As Astley grew older, however, she was grateful for literary companionship provided by women of her own generation. In the 1970s, when writers such as Jolley and Masters began publishing, she was filled with admiration. She had a similar reaction when 35-year-old Helen Garner sprang on to the writing scene in the mid-'70s with *Monkey Grip*, particularly in regard to Garner's ability to portray domesticity and the details of female life with intelligence and poetic wit.

***

Astley's writing room holds a desk and the usual paperwork, but is dominated by an upright piano, which she rarely plays these days. Most of her writing is done in bed at night – scribbling in a notebook with a pen – while her husband listens to the radio. In the mornings after she's had breakfast and washed up, she types up her notes for an hour or two.

A few years ago, she purchased a word processor, but it sat in the house for fourteen months before she summoned the courage to use it.

'It was traumatic', she says. 'I used to look at it sometimes and read the handbook. I mean, the guy came out and gave me lessons, but you know how their hands work, as if they're Fats Waller, like they're playing stride piano. Finally, I rang [writer] Helen Daniel in Melbourne and told her I didn't know how to start a new paragraph. "Press RETURN!" said this voice at the other end. My whole life opened up after that'.

In her forthcoming novel, the narrator comments, 'Anyone who starts from nothing with nothing must be a fanatic. How else create?'

As I mention this, Astley jumps up to do the dishes, which,

she says, are hanging over her like Catholic guilt. As her fast hands sponge the plates, she comments, 'As you know, if you're doing anything, you become quite obsessive, and you think about nothing else.

'I think fiction writing is rather like being an experimental chemist, or an experimental cook. You throw things together and hope some attractive food or drug will emerge. And you hope that it will be a new one, for goodness sake'.

***

At sunset, I stand in her living room, surprised to discover what we have in common. Even though two generations separate us, many of the books on her shelves are also on mine: works by Graham Greene, Christina Stead, Katherine Mansfield, Gabriel Garcia Marquez. When I inspect her CD collection, I'm surprised again by what appears to be our mutual love of jazz. The artists on her rack are also on mine: Ella Fitzgerald, Duke Ellington, Tommy Flanagan, Bill Evans.

And then it seems we have other things in common: her son, Ed, a guitarist, used to do gigs with my musician father in the early 1980s; the original title of her previous novel, *Coda*, was *Mood Indigo*, which she'd had to change at the last minute because I'd already used it as the title of my first book.

When she suggests I choose a CD, I slide out a Johnny Hodges disc and put it on the player. Within moments, she is up off her stool and we are spinning and twirling around the living room. When she asks me to do a tap dance, I perform a quiet soft shoe against the slate tiles of the kitchen and she attempts to follow. After a chorus, we are shuffling and kicking in unison to 'Little Rabbit Blues'.

The next morning, I wake to find her on the verandah, watering pink geraniums. Around the house, a breeze is stealing through the peppermint gums, and the hills beyond are shiny with dew. In spite of the Arcadian dairy country in which she now lives, Astley admits that the landscape doesn't quite inspire her in the same way as her beloved Far North Queensland, which she has so affectionately fictionalised in her books. She and her husband moved to the South Coast ten years ago to be closer to their Sydney-based son. Before that, they lived in the rainforest outside Cairns for a number of years in the '70s and '80s, and it was her experiences there, together with her memories of her early teaching positions in northern outback towns, which have furnished much of the material for her novels.

It is not only the tropical landscape that inspires her, however, but also the outsiders and misfits who populate it. Astley's writing is primarily motivated by anecdotes and yarns, which she collects like a literary bowerbird. 'You do hear remarkable stories up there. And I think one reason is because people are so far away from the centre of government, they can act out their peculiarities.

'I remember one town I was in, the headmaster's wife told me about a circus group that was refused permission to camp near a town. So, during the night, a young man from the circus went to the one haberdashery store in town and broke in and raped the models in the window. And then, when everyone went to work the next morning, they saw these unseemly markings on the front of the floral cotton sundresses. It was told to me with great glee over a supper. I used it in *An Item from the Late News*'.

It almost seems as if Astley continues to write about Queensland in order to negotiate her absence from and deep longing for the weirdness of the north. Certainly, her new novel is overflowing with unforgettable characters, and sensual tropical images. 'I keep going there', she says. 'I can't leave it alone. People say, "Go up there and get a fix, will you?"'

Does she consider herself as a bit of a misfit? Is that why she keeps turning to the far north in both her travels and her fiction? 'Well, I think of myself as boring and dull, but I do like screwballs, yes. I like observing them.'

***

It is now mid-morning, and Astley and I are bowed over another pot of tea. By this time, we've exchanged copies of each other's books. Astley credits the establishment of the Australia Council for the comparative ease with which a young writer can now be published. She maintains that publishers of the '90s are now more willing to publish unknown writers because of endowments they receive from the Literature Board.

'Patronage has been a long-accepted process. People object to it, but Shakespeare was patronised. Since the inception of the Australia Council and the fact that they give financial support to publishing firms to publish books that they think will have some sort of literary cache, I think that has made a great deal of difference to the quality of the writing.

'Life is getting better for writers. And there are all sorts of programs they didn't have thirty or forty years ago. Writers-in-residence at universities, for example'.

In spite of her championing of the Australia Council, Astley has only ever applied for and received one year-long fellowship during her forty-year career. With her customary modesty, she explains she never needed one because she always had a full-time job, that she actually preferred being pressed for time: 'The fact that I had an outside job and was under pressure for time was rather a stimulus. I'd think, "I've got to finish this when I can"'.

Astley is genuinely uncomfortable discussing her own work. She dislikes being interviewed and only relaxes when I turn the tape recorder off. She grows restless and repairs to the verandah for a cigarette, as she has just had the house repainted and doesn't want to stain the walls with smoke. The unbound page proofs of her new novel sit to the right of the teapot, and when I think that it might well be her final novel, I grow sad.

I thumb through the pages. The writing is taut and lyrical, honed by a steady hand.

When she stubs out her cigarette and returns to the room, I ask her if she believes she's getting better the more she writes.

'No', she replies, sitting down. 'I think it was Christopher Koch who said in an interview that once you begin to feel satisfied, that's the beginning of the end. I think you can reach a stage when you're tired. I mean, you're physically tired, because you're physically aged. I think you should learn when to stop'.

I find myself wanting to argue with her, pointing out that Graham Greene continued writing until he was well into his eighties. Astley thinks about it for a moment, and finally agrees.

So is she now working on novel number sixteen?

'I have started one', she admits, sheepishly. 'Only about 5000 words. I've got this great first sentence: "My name is not Francie Massey." Massey is the German word for moderate'.

She asks me what I'm currently writing, and I tell her about the manuscript I've been working on for eleven years, a memoir about my father and me performing on the streets of New York and New Orleans. She nods slowly and says she's often felt as frustrated as I do now, dissatisfied with what she perceives to be her own creative limitations and all the work that must be done to overcome them.

'I often envy painters who can achieve fulfilment with what they're doing in a day, or even half a day, depending on the size [of the painting]. Whereas the sheer plugging away – I mean physically to type out 60–80 000 words – it's a long process. And you can never see the whole thing until you've gone through all this physical yakka'.

When she talks about how vulnerable she feels after she's completed a draft, relief begins to warm my stomach.

'You think, "I'm going to destroy this. I shall burn this now". And then you think, "Oh, I'll tart it up on the second go through".'

It's becoming clear to me that this humour of hers has sustained her through the ups and downs of her writing life. Later on in the day, after she's driven me to the station and hugged me goodbye, I think about the manuscript I can never get right. And what I carry away with me, what I have inherited from Astley, is the quiet knowledge that a significant work of art and a meaningful life are not made quickly or easily.

Sex, Lies and Defamation

(2006)

Editing my memoir *Velocity* was never going to be easy. The interval of time that transpired between the publication of my first volume, *Dreamtime Alice*, in 1998, and the second one, seven years later, had seen the Australian book industry strewn with a messy list of fraudulent memoirists, defamation cases and pulped print runs.

During this period, my own publisher, Random House, suffered dearly: in 1998, Bob Ellis' false claims about the private affairs of Tony Abbott's and Peter Costello's spouses (thirty-three words in a 600-page book) led to the pulping of his political memoir, *Goodbye Jerusalem*, and a $277000 pay-out to the plaintiffs. In 2004, 20000 copies of gangland widow Judith Moran's memoir, *My Story*, had to be pulped, due to complaints lodged by *Age* journalist John Silvester, who objected to Moran's portrayal of his late father in the book. In the same year, these debacles were complicated by the now-infamous Norma Khouri scam. In *Forbidden Love*, the author claimed to have been born and raised in Jordan, to have witnessed the killing of her best friend, Nadia, at the hands of her brutal Muslim father, when in fact she'd grown up in a middle-class Chicago suburb and had a long history of theft and fraud. No wonder my in-house editor, Helen, was nervous.

Velocity is a prequel to my first memoir, ranging, in rough chronological order, from my birth to the age of seventeen, where the second one begins. Some of the more dramatic chapters detail a serial paedophile schoolteacher, a violent, alcoholic, Lebanese lapsed-Muslim stepfather, my widowed aunt who becomes a lesbian in her mid-40s, my twenty-year-old brother marrying my father's fiancée and becoming a Jehovah's Witness. And then there's my mother's hard drinking and depression, her several suicide attempts, the loser boyfriends she'd pick up in bars and clubs, the last of whom was an army chef and small-time crook.

For the sake of authenticity, and to preserve my own sense of recall, I wrote the first draft of *Velocity* with the original names and places intact. I also wrote it with a kind of contrived intention that I would never allow it to be published – not, at least, while my mother was still alive. This trick I played on myself allowed me to write as truthfully as possible, without self-censorship, and without the burden of 'what people would think'. If it were ever contracted to be published, I told myself, I would worry about the consequences then.

The first draft was completed in six months, a record for me, as I am a notoriously slow writer. My first reader was Louis, who is perhaps the toughest critic of my work: ('In your second novel you were treading water … Your third one's a mess until the second half … '). I was expecting something close to this kind of assessment, or worse, but after he finished reading it he was so excited he pressed me to publish it immediately.

Of course, I was ambivalent; my mother, though in ill-health, was still alive, and I certainly didn't want to upset her, in such a frail condition, by dredging up the past. My other problem was that no one else in my family had read the manuscript and the good Catholic girl in me felt torn and slightly devious.

My sister, four years my senior, offered to be my second reader. She had lived with me and my mother until she was fifteen years old and had experienced the majority of the events described in *Velocity*; she is also famously blunt when expressing her opinions, and I knew that if anyone could verify the authenticity of the manuscript, and help me negotiate this ethical quagmire, it would be Lisa.

'I can't comment on the prose style', she said, rather shakily, after having read the work over five consecutive nights. She explained that the experience of reading it unearthed so many forgotten events and mixed emotions that she felt as if she'd relived her entire childhood in the space of a single week.

When we were very young she'd often impersonate a witch – black clothing, wild teased hair – and would announce to me that she had murdered our entire family and was now about to kill me. Her hands would grip my throat, pretending to choke me, until I was an hysterical and blubbering mess, begging her to spare me, after which time she'd loosen her hold and drop the ruse entirely. She repeated this threat for several years – and each time I'd fall for it – until I was in the second grade and old enough to call her bluff.

As I discussed the manuscript of *Velocity* with her, I asked her if I'd exaggerated or unintentionally misrepresented any characters or events. 'No', she replied, 'it's spot-on'. She paused and drew in her breath. 'Though I don't think I tried to kill you *that* much'.

Her next comment was made with much more confidence: 'Go ahead and publish it', she advised. 'Mum won't even read it'. I was unsure about this, as I knew she had read all my previous books. I didn't know what my mother had thought of my first memoir, *Dreamtime Alice*, as she'd never acknowledged to me that it even existed. 'Yes', argued my sister, 'that's because you gave her copies. If you don't mention the fact that you've published a new memoir, she'll never know'.

I pondered this line of reasoning, and the more I thought about it, the more it made sense. At the time, my mother was living an extremely reclusive life – she no longer left her Carlton home at all. Her only contact with the outside world was through her television set, and through her schizophrenic neighbour, Beryl, who visited once a week and did her banking and paid her bills. I concluded that as long as I stayed off her favourite television program, *The Bert Newton Show*, during the publicity, she would have no idea what I'd published.

Buoyed by the support of my husband and sister, I submitted the manuscript to my publisher in August of 2004. After it was accepted, it was forwarded to a freelance editor, who did the usual tidying up: consistency, spelling, grammar. She helped me tighten up the time line when it became elastic or too vague. There were, however, no structural changes.

The manuscript was then forwarded to an in-house editor, who was responsible for anticipating any legal problems and eliminating them prior to publication. The last thing Random House wanted, on the heels of Bob Ellis and Judith Moran, was another lawsuit.

After reading the edit, Helen, my in-house editor, told me it was a potential minefield of defamation. She and Random's lawyers spent weeks combing through every sentence, and with each round of proofs I had to change more names, disguise more locations, and further verify certain events. There were four aspects of the work Helen was most concerned about. The first was the paedophile teacher (*Did he really have a birthmark on his hand? Did he really own a caravan?*); the second was an anecdote about my drummer father being on tour with Little Richard and discovering him in his hotel room 'having a wank' (*This definitely has to go. Did you know that Little Richard is very religious?*); the third was the possible reaction of my mother (*What is she going to think? Suicide attempts, fucking around ... Surely she'll try and sue us!*); the fourth and most drawn-out controversy was in regard to the third chapter, in which my mother takes a live-in housekeeping job for a family who owned a hotel in the outer Western suburbs of Sydney. It was after my parents had separated and my sister and I went with her to live at the hotel. The husband-and-wife owners also bred thoroughbred racehorses and Great Danes. The husband was a bloated, slovenly tyrant. The three young sons, whom my mother was hired to look after, were merely smaller, thinner versions of their father. It was one of the most trying years of her life.

Disguising the paedophile teacher was easy: I changed the location of his home, his school, his holiday house, the names of his various victims (except, of course, my own). His name, the colour of his hair, the subjects he taught were all transformed. But the core of the teacher's personality – his patterns of behaviour, his voice, his seduction techniques remained intact. None of the actual events were toned down or removed.

The saga of Little Richard was drawn out for weeks. I wanted desperately to keep the anecdote in; my editor and the lawyers, however, would not budge on this point. I argued that it was common knowledge that the singer was a compulsive masturbator and had a history of homosexuality. Helen would not budge: *That's not enough to cover us.*

When the second round of page proofs arrived in February, the passage was removed completely, and as I re-read that particular section I felt as if I'd suddenly lost a limb. It just didn't read well; the transitions were clumsy; the chapter had lost its delicate dovetailing of incident.

Realising how upset and irritable I was becoming, Louis quietly came to my rescue. A compulsive bibliophile, he trawled through all his search engines on the net, discovered a second-hand copy of Little Richard's autobiography tucked away in a small bookstore in Macon, Georgia, and had it express-mailed to Sydney within three days. Just before we went to print with *Velocity* I had the pleasure of reading out the following excerpt from the book in front of all the editors at Random House:

My whole gay activities were really into masturbation. I
used to do it six or seven times a day. In fact everybody used
to tell me that I should get a trophy for it, I did it so much.
I got to be a professional jack-offer. I would do it just to be

doing something … Felt bad after I did it though. I'd always be mad after I finished … Most gay people fall in love with themselves.

My father's anecdote was immediately restored to the page proofs and I enjoyed the sly, victorious feeling of someone who has just won a high-odds bet.

Since the publication of *Velocity*, many reviewers and critics have commented on the significance of the fact that my father is referred to as 'Gerry' in the book, while my mother remains 'nameless'. Various theories on the reason for this have been speculated in interviews and articles: I was obviously closer to my father than my mother and I underscored this dynamic by the familiarity of 'Gerry' as opposed to the formality of 'my mother'; the mother figure is portrayed as a shadowy and unfathomable presence in the book and hence the absence of her name reflects this ambiguity; and finally (and this one is a big stretch), I'm making some sort of feminist 'point' about the universality of the female experience and decided to leave her nameless.

The reason, in fact, was purely practical. Before the advance review copies were printed in February, which were the second and penultimate set of page proofs, my nervous editor, without my permission, removed all references to my mother's actual name (Helen was not convinced that my mother would remain oblivious to the publication of *Velocity*, despite my anecdote about her reclusiveness and my intention to stay off *The Bert Newton Show*).

My only concern with regard to my mother was that I mention in the book that she collected a deserted wife's pension while still living with my father, then my stepfather, for a total of five years. I didn't want to cause her any legal problems, let alone have her being fined for fraud and held responsible for repaying the total amount. The lawyer assured me the likelihood of that happening was so remote it was negligible. The story of the pension stayed in.

Six weeks before the publication date I received the final set of page proofs. I was about to sit down and read them for the last time when the phone rang. My younger brother was on the line. His voice was shaky. Our mother had been admitted to hospital, suffering respiratory problems.

Fourteen hours later, she simply stopped breathing.

I packed some clothes and my page proofs and flew down to Melbourne to make the funeral arrangements. Of course, I was grieving, but I also felt guilty and divided: had she decided to die before the memoir was published? Had I, in some indirect way, inadvertently killed her? I had to shake myself out of these grim digressions – she'd had absolutely no idea that I'd written the memoir, let alone its publication date.

It was, I told myself, just a spooky coincidence.

***

Two days after the funeral, I sat at her dining room table and began reading through the final set of proofs. Now that my mother was gone, I could now at least restore her name to the book. As the sun went down, I enjoyed writing *Betty*, *Betty*, *Betty*, back into the proofs.

'No', wailed my editor, when I later spoke with her on the phone. 'You can't put her name back in. Other people could identify themselves in the text through her name'. I realised she was just doing her job, but I was now exasperated. Everyone else in the family is named correctly in the book and I silently cursed Bob Ellis and Judith Moran for creating such a climate of fear and paranoia. Finally, my editor's boss weighed in on the debate: my mother's name was allowed to stay in.

There was a last-minute flurry of legal checks before the proofs went to print. Fortunately, many of the shady characters in the memoir have long since passed away. The chapter set in the Mulga Hotel (originally called the Hotel Namatjira), where my mother had been a housekeeper in the early '70s, required the most work, mainly because it paints an unflattering portrait of my mother's former boss: 'Balding, bug-eyed and extremely overweight, he had the apoplectic face of a heavy drinker and teeth the colour of wet cement...' Every sentence he uttered contained an expletive. 'I told you fucking kids not to feed the fucking horses. Roving Eye's put on fucking weight. Now, which one of you little bastards did it? I wanna fucking know!' The setting for the chapter changed from Rooty Hill, to Mount Druitt, to finally a nondescript, anonymous suburb in Sydney's outer west. The hotel was no longer flanked by a railway line. I had to change the colour of Mrs Ronson's hair from chestnut to red. Her three sons also had to have fictional red hair. The real Mrs Ronson had a large, natural beauty spot on her cheek that had to be removed when she became a character in my memoir. When my editor realised that the names of Ronson's racehorses and Great Danes were original, these, too, had to be changed. It started to become ludicrous when I had to fictionalise the colour of the walls and the pattern of their living room carpet. All this to avoid recognition and, ergo, possible litigation.

Two months after the book was published, as I was preparing to attend the Byron Bay Writers' Festival, I was shocked to receive an email from the 'real' Mrs Ronson. I hadn't heard from her since the day her husband had unceremoniously sacked my mother, over thirty-three years ago.

Dear Mandy,
We have been looking forward to your arrival in Byron as
we are following your career with much admiration and
would love to meet you after all these years. We realise you
shall be very busy but maybe you could see us on Saturday or
whenever it suits to sign our books ... Hoping you will oblige.
Best wishes,
Margaret Tyler (AKA Ronson)

***

Initially, I was wary. Why did the Tylers want to see me? Surely they would take issue with my portrait of their family, or, even worse, threaten to sue me for defamation? Louis calmed me down and urged me to ring them, which I did. Margaret's voice was soft and girlish on the phone. She giggled like a nine-year-old and was thrilled to hear from me. I arranged to meet her and the two younger sons for lunch on a Saturday afternoon.

At the restaurant, as Louis and I waited for them to arrive, I nervously gulped my beer. Margaret swept into view first, wearing a fashionable black-and-white jacket, her fingers glittering with rings. She threw her arms around me and pecked me on both cheeks. She was now in her early sixties, but the beauty spot I had excised from her face in the memoir was still there, above her right lip, exactly as I'd remembered it. Her two sons, in their early forties, followed. I'd described them in *Velocity* as rude, spiteful boys: setting fires in the garden, exposing their genitals to me over breakfast, slipping laxatives into the drinks of guests. I was stunned to receive hugs and kisses from them, too, as if I'd bestowed upon them some kind of honour.

Over lunch, Margaret tossed her hair over her shoulder and admired the accuracy of the descriptions of her late husband, Phil: 'He really DID have teeth the colour of wet cement. And it's true, he couldn't complete a sentence without swearing!' She burst out again in rapturous, girlish laughter. I began to relax. The sons nodded in agreement. It was only then that I realised that the boys had hated their father even more than I had, and my descriptions of him were now providing them with a kind of solace. Instead of offending them, I could see now that I had managed to articulate in public what Margaret and her sons could only admit to each other in private. Not only were they happy to be portrayed as such in *Velocity*, by the end of the lunch the three of them were insisting that, when a new edition is published, I restore their real names, and also that of their former hotel and its location.

Margaret had a copy of each of my books in her bag. She pulled them out and, like a proud stage mother, insisted that I sign them. 'It's important we all stay in touch from now on', she declared, gesturing at the books, 'because this is all part of our history'. She then invited me and Louis to her home the following day for lunch. Before leaving, she picked up the bill.

Margaret always wanted a daughter and she now rings me frequently to chat or ask my advice about her sons. And since I've lost my mother, the arrangement works well for me, too. Instead of being sued, I now have a new best friend.

In Ernest:
Hemingway and the
Art of the Story

(2001)

During the past four or five decades, the popularity of Hemingway's fiction has waned, especially with writers, readers and women of my generation, whose feminist and post-feminist tastes lean away from what is perceived to be stories of violence, sport and masculine authority. His women are weak and manipulative. He relies on exotic settings and situations to shoulder the drama of his stories. He is out of fashion these days because he was rumoured to be homophobic, anti-Semitic, a bad drunk, a womaniser. Hemingway, it seems, only wrote of horseracing, fishing, boxing and skiing – and people have decided not to read him as the work seems so macho and dated.

In interviews, when I mention that one of my favourite short story writers is Hemingway, invariably there is an awkward pause, and often a bemused reaction. Surely I would name someone more fashionable: Alice Munro, maybe, or Lorrie Moore. My reply is always that Hemingway's best work is important because he crafted a style and tone that approximated his ongoing themes and subject matter. For that alone he is worth reading.

'The dignity and movement of an iceberg', he once remarked, 'is due to only one-eighth of it being above water'. This simple statement aptly reflects Hemingway's aesthetic and thematic concerns. He was one of the first short story writers to pare back subjectivity and exposition to the extent that people had to read actively – indeed, they had to enter the narrative in order to fathom the seven-eighths of the story the author deliberately omitted. It is through his silences that Hemingway expressed the most, like a jazz musician always knowing what notes not to play. 'A writer may omit things that he knows', he said, 'and the reader, if the writer is writing truly enough, will have a feeling of those things as strongly as though the writer had stated them'. This technique is often referred to as Hemingway's 'objective' style, in which the point of view avoids analysis of a character's thoughts and feelings and instead creates external actions, images and settings that suggest the inner life of a character without explanation or commentary. As the American author Frederick Busch remarked on the ending of *A Farewell to Arms*: 'He doesn't have to tell me outright that Henry weeps for his Catherine; the way he excludes the tears makes me taste them.' In this sense, the most minimal of Hemingway's stories are probably closer to the genres of poetry and playwriting.

He did, however, find his antecedents in Chekhov, whose voice, if you listen hard enough, can be heard below the surface of Hemingway's prose. Chekhov was a master at using objective external details to convey complex emotional states, and employed understatement and irony to further the drama of the story. The rendering of the internal through the external, the subjective through the objective, is a technique that TS Eliot later described as the 'objective correlative'.

This is one of the primary reasons Chekhov was hailed as the father of the modern short story, but most critics and readers of his prose forget that Chekhov was an accomplished playwright, and I suspect his discovery of narrative distance in the short story was as much a consequence of his writing for the theatre as his desire to explore new narrative forms. His first two collections, *Tales of*

Melpomene (1884) and *Motley Tales* (1886), were considered by critics to be light and frivolous. It wasn't until 1887, when he published *In the Twilight*, that Chekhov attracted recognition as a virtuoso of the short story form. It was also in 1887 that Chekhov's first play, *Ivanov*, opened. Chekhov appears to have developed the objective (dramatic) point of view in his short stories concurrently with his first works for theatre. 'Subjectivity is a terrible thing', he once said. 'It is bad in this alone, that it reveals the author's hands and feet ... Best of all is to avoid depicting the hero's state of mind; you ought to try and make it clear from the hero's actions'. These are the words of a playwright rather than a prose writer, for the only tools the former has in order to convey meaning are dialogue, action and setting – the three things both Chekhov and Hemingway concentrated on in order to suggest emotional and psychological undercurrents. Chekhov and Hemingway wanted readers to bring to the story what an actor would when reading a script: engagement, interpretation, a layer of interiority in order to bring the work to life, a process during which the reader – like the thespian – becomes a collaborator in the making of meaning and experience.

It was Hemingway in particular who mastered, in prose form, the playwright's technique of conveying exposition through minimal dialogue, of 'showing' rather than 'telling'. Many of his settings appear to be influenced by the obvious limitations of the theatre: one scene, one symbolic background, whether it be the café of 'A Clean, Well-lighted Place', the railway station of 'Hills Like White Elephants', or the single train compartment of 'A Canary for One'. His most elliptical stories resemble one-act plays, comprised of dialogue, minimal action and single settings that function as thematic keys. In 'Hills Like White Elephants', for example, a quarrelling couple sits on a railway station 'between two lines of rails in the sun'. In fact, the station is a junction, a crossroad, and perfectly represents the emotional crossroads of the man and the woman, who, we sense, will never be going in the same direction again. Hemingway inherited the distant, dramatic style from Chekhov and, to a lesser extent, from Joyce. As Charles May notes: 'What at first seems merely a realistic depiction of ordinary physical reality communicates metaphorically what is, basically, incommunicable.'

Hemingway's iceberg aesthetic extends even further than his point of view and style, than the clipped dialogue and spareness of the prose. Often, that which is incommunicable or unknowable is the very subject of the story, as if the protagonist is standing on a small, frozen island and gazing into the depths of the surrounding water at his own terrible darkness. This is why 'A Clean, Well-Lighted Place' is one of Hemingway's best-known stories, and why he felt it to be one of his most successful. It is probably not much longer than 700 words; it is a single scene, and in it very little 'happens'. The 'place' of the title is a Spanish café, and by the end of the story, the cleanliness, the light and the order of the café provide a safe and comforting protection against the unknown – the darkness and danger of night.

There are only three characters in the story, an ageing waiter, a much younger waiter and an old man who drinks brandy long into the night, as he does every night. The tension is mainly between the waiters: the older one doesn't mind keeping the café open; the younger one wants to close up and go home. The customer, however, won't leave and continues to drink brandy. It is the older waiter who intuits the man's need to stay every evening and get drunk in the bar, his need for 'a light in the night'.

The silent understanding that exists between the drinker and the older waiter is underscored by the opening dialogue, in which the younger waiter comments on the fact that the brandy-drinker had tried to commit suicide the week before. When the older waiter asks why, the younger one says, 'He was in despair.' When asked what caused the despair, the younger replies, 'Nothing.' When asked, 'How do you know it was nothing?' the younger comments, 'He has plenty of money.' As critic Carlos Baker points out, the force of this story is gathered through understatement, hints, the subtext of details and dialogue, and the transformation of 'the young waiter's mere *nothing* into the old waiter's Something – a Something called Nothing which is so huge, terrible, overbearing, and inevitable and omnipresent that, once experienced, it can never be forgotten'. The antidote to the Nothing that is Something is the small cocoon – the safe fraction of iceberg that stands above the sea of darkness – the place that is the clean, well-lighted café.

Death (*nada*) is at the heart of many of Hemingway's short stories, either literally or figuratively. I suspect this is why in recent times there has been a certain amount of confusion about Hemingway's work, along with the misconception that he only writes about bull fights, hunting, boxing and masculine heroics – actions that result in the protagonist stoically facing a violent and tragic end. A measured reading of his stories doesn't support this summary. Very few of them are, in fact, sports-related. Most appear modest and deceptively simple, relying on dialogue, patterns of detail and their underlying subtexts to create the drama, rather than celebrating gratuitous violence. What many readers fail to recognise is that, even in the stories of violence, Hemingway uses sport as a narrative occasion to explore his literary obsession with the Nothing that is Something, just as he used the simple device of the waiters in the café of 'A Clean, Well-Lighted Place'.

The three stories I shall concentrate on in this essay – 'Hills Like White Elephants', 'A Canary for One' and 'The Short Happy Life of Francis Macomber' – are concerned with the complexities of male/female relationships. In these stories the *nada* concept is realised through breakdowns in partnerships – death comes in the form of separation, divorce, or simply a couple's inability to communicate.

Following Chekhov's dictum that the short story should begin in the middle of things, each opens in a drama that has begun long before we are admitted into it. There is an unspoken 'it' in all of them, a buried subject that the characters talk around but do not directly address. 'The Short Happy Life of Francis Macomber' begins: 'It was now lunch time and they were all sitting under the double green fly of the dining tent pretending that nothing had happened.' Set in the wilds of Africa during a safari, the mysterious 'it' is not directly explained until a quarter of a way through the story. The experience of reading the story up until that point is one that evokes a certain voyeuristic quality, as if the reader were eavesdropping on some vastly personal subject.

Hemingway begins similarly in 'Hills Like White Elephants'. After the two characters have been established in the symbolic setting of the Spanish railway station, the man, who is never named, remarks, 'It's really an awfully simple operation, Jig ... It's not really an operation at all.' In 'Hills', Hemingway pushed his elliptical style further and the characters never directly reveal what 'it' is. The conversation progresses: 'It's the only thing that's made us unhappy.'; 'If I do it you won't ever worry?'; and, ' ... once they take it away, you never get it back.' A close reading of the story reveals, entirely through inference, that the man is trying to persuade the woman to have an abortion; she in turn does not exactly refuse or agree; her main desire is for the man to want what he does not, to find Something in Nothing. This idea is reinforced in the title, by a seemingly casual observation the girl makes, that the hills near the station look like white elephants. White elephants, of course, are either associated with totally useless possessions or a possession that is a liability because the expense of keeping it far outweighs its value. After the girl begs the man to drop the subject ('Would you please please please please please please stop talking?'), Hemingway can't resist invoking the *nada* concept in the last line of the story: 'I feel fine,' she said. 'There's nothing wrong with me. I feel fine.' Nothing is exactly resolved, but by the end of the story we know that, figuratively at least, these two won't be travelling on the same train for long.

In 'Canary for One' the Nothing that is Something is not revealed until the last line of the story. An American couple is travelling between Cannes and the Gare de Lyon in Paris, sharing a compartment with a partially deaf woman, also American, who carries with her a caged canary. Through seemingly insignificant dialogue the woman reveals that the canary is a gift to her daughter, a kind of consolation prize for the loss of the Swiss man the girl had wished to marry originally. The mother forbade the union because, as she maintains, 'American men make the best husbands.' The woman soon discovers that the couple is American, and throughout the story she twitters at them more frequently than the bird, particularly about virtues of American husbands. The train compartment functions as a cage confining the three characters, all of whom gaze out at the world through the window. The point of view of the story is a very distant third-person singular, from the American man's perspective – though, typically, the fact that he is narrating is not revealed until halfway through the story, when he remarks, 'For several minutes I had not listened to the American lady, who was talking to my wife.'

The story begins with an image of domestic comfort: 'The train passed very quickly a long, red stone house with a garden and four thick palm trees with tables underneath them in the shade.' Soon, this image is undercut by another, more sinister, sight of domesticity, which foreshadows the last line of the story: 'As it was getting dark the train passed a farmhouse in a burning field. Motor-cars were stopped along the road and bedding and things from inside the farmhouse were spread in the field.' A similar juxtaposition is created between the very fast train the three are travelling on – which the older woman is convinced will crash – and the image the man observes just before they arrive in Paris: 'We were passing three cars that had been in a wreck. They were splintered open and the roof sagged in.' At the end of the story, the older woman walks away down the platform with her canary, convinced the couple she is leaving is happy because they're both Americans. The last line of the story, however, reveals that the couple's Nothing (what the narrator has failed to tell us) is definitely Something: 'We were returning to Paris to set up separate residences.' The line functions as a dramatic punch line – deadpan, ironic. Most of the story, it seems, will happen after it has ended.

***

Hemingway's various techniques for communicating the incommunicable have a lot to offer writers at any stage of their careers. Not to read him because he was too macho, or too violent, or too sexist is to miss out on a consummate craftsman who honed his work into a precise marriage of style and subject matter. He was a writer who made silence sing, who found a way to disturb readers by what he chose to leave out.

True, I am not always comfortable with his manipulative women, his emasculated men, his tragic heroes, but I admire and have been inspired by the way in which he wrote about them. In the late 1990s, I decided to have a dialogue with Hemingway's stories in three of my own, inspired by 'Hills Like White Elephants', 'The Short Happy Life of Francis Macomber', and, to a lesser extent, 'A Canary for One'.

Employing his signature iceberg technique, in which seven-eighths of the story is known only to the writer, I wrote 'Still Life' as a way of conversing with 'Hills Like White Elephants'. In an unnamed beachside café in Sydney, a couple discusses a serious problem they share, but without ever directly naming it. Just as the hills and what they resemble in Hemingway's story provide a metaphorical key to the subject – the unborn child – in 'Still Life', the objective correlative here is the beach across the road, usually a favourite for surfers, though on this particular day the sea is uncommonly flat and still.

My couple, too, is in transition, as they have been travelling by bus from northern NSW and have stopped off in Sydney for the afternoon before continuing down to Melbourne. Their relationship is also in transition, and seems to be going down (heading south) rather quickly. In my story, however, it is the woman who broaches the delicate, unnamed threat to their union, the *nada* that lurks between them. After ordering lunch, she remarks to her lover, 'Maybe if you went to see someone … It's pretty common, you know … More common than what you'd think.' When she receives no response, she adds, 'I could go with you … We could go together.'

The 'it', however, remains elusive, drawing more and more attention to itself because the subject remains unnamed. The man tries to distract the woman from addressing the *nada* by remarking that 'the surf might get up' and later they could go for a swim. The woman replies, rather testily, that it has been predicted that the surf will not get up today and thus there is no point in swimming. The two talk around the subject and gradually, through inferences and verbal slips – 'Maybe it's psychological'; 'It affects us both' – it is suggested that the woman is trying to talk the man into seeking medical help for his impotence – a condition that is realised symbolically by the beach across the road that has no surf.

The inspiration for this story came not only from 'Hills Like White Elephants', but also from the American painter Edward Hopper. I have always been drawn to his paintings for the same reason I admire the short stories of Ernest Hemingway – he composed figures centred in auras of mystery, and gazing at them afforded the viewer a certain voyeuristic experience. Hemingway makes you feel as if you're eavesdropping all the time; Hopper makes you feel as if you're perving all the time. He positions the viewer as a peeping Tom, and you find yourself experiencing the usually hidden tensions between men and women, without ever knowing the cause. Hopper's images speak of an unnameable loneliness and isolation, and in paintings such as *Hotel by a Railroad*, *Hotel Lobby*, and *New York Movie* the loneliness is not individual only, but an expression of disconnection between lovers – articulated through their tense bodies and expressions, in the ways in which they always turn away from each other. In this sense, Hopper also communicates the incommunicable. His preoccupation with the confined spaces of hotel rooms, lobbies and cafés is a visual equivalent of the spatially limited railway stations, bars and trains that are signature settings of Hemingway's stories. Both writer and painter found resonance in these public settings of transience. (In researching Hopper's work for this essay, I was not surprised to find that Hopper was a huge fan of Hemingway, and wrote to him frequently.)

I've often felt that the painting that best reflects Hemingway's aesthetic was Hopper's *Nighthawks*, which is also his most famous. In many ways it can be interpreted as a visual relative of 'A Clean, Well-Lighted Place' and 'Hills Like White Elephants'. For this reason, when drafting 'Still Life', I decided to have a print of *Nighthawks* hanging on the wall of the beachside café. Approximating Chekhov's and Hemingway's third-person distant narrative point of view, the narrator describes the famous painting:

> A man and a woman were sitting up at the wooden counter
> of an American diner. The man looked like Humphrey
> Bogart and wore a suit and hat. He held a cigarette between
> his fingers. The woman, also smoking, was pretty and wore
> a red dress. They were both drinking coffee. It was night …
> There were two other figures in the painting. An attendant in
> white stood behind the curved wooden counter. His lips were
> parted, as though he were answering a question the Bogart
> look-alike had asked. The fourth figure sat at the other end
> of the counter with his back to the viewer. His suit was the
> same greyish-blue as the first man's, the one who sat with the
> woman in the red dress.

The couple in the 'Still Life' story find themselves in a startlingly similar situation: they are the only people in the café apart from the waiter and a man dining nearby. Since the two are unable to address directly the source of their own personal *nada* – the man's impotence – they both use their individual interpretations as a way of talking about what they cannot say. Each makes predictions about the couple in the painting as a way of second-guessing the other's intentions and beliefs:

> They look serious ... They've been having an affair. See the way she can't look him in the eye?
>
> She's contemplating her cigarette. They've probably just had sex.
>
> Is that all you ever think about ... The woman in the painting ... she's going to leave him. She just hasn't found a way of telling him.
>
> Maybe if you didn't drink so much—
>
> Don't you think ... that he's trying to talk that woman into something she really doesn't want to do?

The couple continue to argue about aesthetics as a way of articulating the unspeakable. The man maintains he loves the way Hopper 'leaves just enough out to make it interesting', how everything is 'just below the surface', while the woman, frustrated by what is left out, maintains that 'even when he paints a couple, there's always this huge distance between them, like so much hasn't been said.'

The man distracts the woman by continuing to suggest that 'the surf might get up' despite radio reports predicting the opposite. The woman comments, 'You know I don't like swimming if there's no surf.' In this story, like 'Hills', nothing is resolved on a literal level, but the reader probably senses that in their silences the union, like that of the couple in the painting, will never be the same again. 'Still Life' employs many of the objective techniques of 'Hills', but slants the story toward an opposite, more 'female' point of view: it is the man who has changed physically, not the woman, and it is she who tried to persuade him to restore their former – but unattainable – harmony. 'Still Life' is not so much a feminist revision of 'Hills' as a second voice to it, a literary dialogue.

My thoughts about Hemingway and literary dialogues have had an influence on other short stories in my collection, *Fifteen Kinds of Desire* (2001). 'The Drover's Wife', for example, is a narrative improvisation on the other Drover versions – first authored by Henry Lawson in 1892, then reworked and parodied by Murray Bail in 1975, in a story that 'dialogues' in turn with the painting *The Drover's Wife*, by Russell Drysdale. I've also reimagined several fairytales – all set in Sydney's red-light district, Kings Cross, which functions as a contemporary version of Grimms' deep, dark woods. The story 'Ash' is a reworking of 'Cinderella', in which the protagonist is a seventeen-year-old boy, who is still a virgin. Ash is forced to work as a receptionist in his stepfather's brothel after his mother has died. In 'The Best', which is a reworking of 'Snow White', the same boy is expelled from the brothel and his stepfather's home after he is discovered stealing from the till. In order to support himself he becomes a transvestite prostitute on William Street. His life is threatened by an older, more experienced transsexual hooker on the same block, who was considered the best and the prettiest, until seven English backpackers take pity on Ash and cart him back to their nearby hostel. In 'Beau', which is a rewriting of 'Sleeping Beauty', a mother of three boys is hit by a car and falls into a permanent coma. 'Scarlet' is a reworking of 'Little Red Riding Hood', in which the protagonist is the eleven-year-old daughter of a heroin dealer who lives in Kings Cross. Scarlet has been taught how to mix heroin and inject it into her mother's veins in the event that her mother is too strung out to do it herself. Instead of being a cautionary tale about a young girl too naïve to protect herself, it becomes a parable that makes a virtue out of knowingness: the danger and corruption with which Scarlet has been raised proves to be her best defence during her walk through the 'woods', which are the threatening streets of Kings Cross.

My dialogues with the original stories and fairytales are inspired by the spirit of revisionism, although, unlike the revisionist fictions of Angela Carter or Margaret Atwood, my references to the original texts are unobtrusive; I've been told that they're not apparent during a first reading. The stories in *Fifteen Kinds of Desire* contain no direct quotations or replications, but invert and play with the subject matter and form of the 'master narratives'. With these stories, I do not see myself arguing with the original texts; rather, the conversation is between me and the ways in which women and men have been imagined. Much of what we communicate to one another remains underneath the storyline, in the silences that Hemingway taught me not to fill.

Satirists of Suburbia: Mrs Edna Everage Paints John Brack

(2007)

In the late '60s, Barry Humphries approached Melbourne artist John Brack and asked him to paint a portrait of Humphries' theatrical alter ego, Edna Everage. At the time, Humphries was an entertainer in his late twenties, enjoying great early success on the stage. He was such a flamboyant alcoholic, however, that he would soon be committed to a Melbourne mental institution for twelve months. Brack, on the other hand, was a middle-aged recluse. Because he was unable to make a living from his work he was forced to teach full-time. He was also an introspective man who led a deliberately boring life in order to focus on his art. On the surface, these two misfits didn't seem to have much in common.

'You've got to paint Edna', Humphries insisted. 'You're the perfect artist'. Brack, apparently, let out a long, low groan, as if he'd been asked to paint something as inexplicable as an odour, or a breeze. Yet Humphries, who considered himself an accomplished landscape painter and collector of art, continued to press the curmudgeonly Brack until he finally acquiesced.

Curiously, Humphries did not want himself painted. Had he wished for that, he might have gone elsewhere. After having sat for a portrait by Brack, most subjects were horrified by the outcomes, which is probably why he painted so few of them during his sixty-year career. 'I never flattered them', admits Brack. 'I always felt my portraits were truthful accounts of the sitters, but they nearly all felt otherwise. I think most of them hated their portraits – Sir Garfield Barwick certainly did – though some were too polite to say so'.

Perhaps that's the first reason why Humphries chose Brack. Mrs Edna Everage – as she was known in the '60s – has been described by fans as Humphries' alter ego and an impersonation of his difficult and demanding mother. But I suspect Edna is simply a vehicle that allows Humphries to express all the 'naughty' observations that the polite and mannered Barry never allows himself to utter.

In spite of his reputation as an introvert, Brack, too, had a rather wicked sense of humour that erupted when he kept the right company. But what the entertainer and the painter had most in common was their gift for satire, particularly when the subject was Australian suburbia. While Humphries, in the guise of Edna, teased and poked fun at middle-class monotony – her husband is called 'Norm' and her surname is a pun on the people who are perpetually Average – Brack's visual mythology is built upon images that resonate with suburban conformity. Some, like *The Car*, are whimsical and funny; others, like his famous *Collins St., 5pm* – which portrays grim-faced, uniformly bored and boring office workers moving like a herd of sheep along the footpath – are coruscating comments on the bland, unquestioning rituals of everyday people.

Early on, both entertainer and painter were influenced by literature. As a young man, Brack initially wished to be a poet. It wasn't until he saw Van Gogh's painting *The Night Café* in a shop window in Little Collins Street that he decided he wanted to paint. He admits the image had an enormous impact upon him, and changed his life forever. As an adolescent in suburban Melbourne, Humphries wrote poetry and short stories on his father's typewriter and posted them off to a children's show on ABC Radio for broadcast. At fourteen, he was already an avid collector of second-hand and rare books, printing his own ex-libris bookplates to paste onto the inside covers. In his twenties, he became an accomplished watercolourist and collector of fine art and classical music. Both men, having grown up in suburban middle-class Melbourne, embraced literature and art as a way of transcending the mind-numbing conformity – the norm, the average, the monotony of post-war Australia.

It is has been said that there are two kinds of artists in the world: the first confirms society and works well within it; the second upsets the status quo and their best work is created in opposition to the dominant culture in which they live. There is no doubt that these two men fall into the latter category, particularly Brack. In fact, in 1980, when his paintings began selling after decades of commercial failure, the hermetic artist felt anxious and sullied, as if public acceptance and social adoration equalled some deficit in his work. 'Suddenly, at age sixty', he once said in an interview, 'I was the big success; people were clamouring for the next picture, the next show; prices shot away. I felt there was something wrong. If I'm going to be so popular, I feel uneasy, so I must paint a picture that is A) unpopular and B) unsaleable'.

At the time Humphries requested the portrait, Brack had recently resigned from his position as head of the National Gallery School and for the first time in his life was able to devote himself entirely to painting. He began working on a series that would go on to define his visual style and artistic preoccupations. Based on ballroom dancers, all the figures in the series are trapped in difficult, ritualised poses. Brack painted numbers on their backs, suggesting a lack of individuality, and as the viewer imagines them repeating the same steps over and over they acquire the air of robots or prisoners, rather than joyful human beings. The forced smiles, the uniform suits, the similar '60s dresses illuminate the repetitive routines of everyday lives. But unlike his earlier painting *Collins St.,*

5pm, in which Brack portrays his subjects as unquestioning and numb, the ballroom series is graced with a sense of empathy. The dancers are portrayed in precarious positions, almost to the point of collapsing onto the slippery polished floor, suggesting the fine balancing act that is contemporary human existence. 'I see the twentieth-century world as being in a state of precarious balance', Brack once observed. 'Things are on the verge of toppling, but they haven't quite yet'. Finally, the series attempts to capture the subtextual truth of fabrication. It is in this quest that the careers of Brack and Humphries intersect, for the young entertainer, too, was preoccupied with the very same subject. In the guise of Mrs Edna Everage, Humphries was – and still is – trying to tell the truth about the human facade. Both painter and entertainer embrace and celebrate the ironies of artifice.

In contrast to Humphries' wild, on-stage improvisations, Brack was a measured and self-conscious artist. He had to contemplate his subject deeply before beginning a painting, always making water-colour and pen-and-ink studies on paper, adjusting and rearranging the composition. He has admitted that he often felt terrified the moment before he applied the initial brushstroke of a new work, and frequently postponed that first step for days.

Perhaps he felt even more terror than usual when he was faced with Edna, as the task before him was not only to paint a portrait of a woman, but the man behind the mask. When composing portraiture, Brack not only attempted to portray the physical characteristics of the sitter, but the psychological state as well. Humphries remembers, as he was dressed as Edna and posing for the portrait, that Brack was absolutely meticulous while he worked and hence often dissatisfied with the progress of the portrait. 'Oh, this is hideous, this is horrible!' Brack would cry over and over. To which Humphries would reply, 'That's good, keep at it!'

***

When I look at *An image of Barry Humphries in the character of Mrs Everage* now, I can see many of Brack's preoccupations and themes embedded in the composition. The artist's fascination with artifice is immediately obvious in his choice of colour. The neon pinks and greens are unnatural – almost kitsch – and suggest the fabric of Edna's ensemble is probably made from that equally unnatural fabric so popular in the 1960s – nylon. The only flowers in the painting are also artificial: the ridiculously blue blossoms that crown Edna's head, for example, the flap of which points like an arrow towards the floral pattern of the settee.

Both artist and entertainer were compelled to portray average people trapped in unquestioning rituals, and this compulsion is also realised in Edna's choice of jewellery, and the way she has composed herself. The imitation pearls are so tight they are almost a yoke or a collar around the neck of the man inside the disguise, while the bracelets around her wrist can be viewed as glittering handcuffs anchoring Edna's right gloved hand to her left. The rest of her body is weighted against the pattern of suburbia embedded in the floral design of the settee.

There are virtually no vertical or horizontal lines in the portrait; it is largely composed of repeating circular rhythms, from the settee's upholstery, the curve of Edna's back, the pearls and bracelet, the glasses, the creases in the gloves and clothes, the blossoming blue wreath around her head. The only true vertical lines can be found when one looks beyond the facade of the average Mrs Everage, to find the true features of the individual behind it: the man Barry Humphries. The unmistakable cleft of Barry's chin, the spaces between his teeth, the slight crease between his eyes, the individual strands of his long brown hair. Later, Humphries would adopt an outrageous purple wig when impersonating Edna, but back in the '60s, both he and his alter ego shared the same brown bob parted down the middle of the head. The only other vertical line is the corner of the room, which seems to be spearing the crown of Edna's head and creates the visual and metaphorical spine of the portrait: Mrs Everage is literally and figuratively 'in a corner', walled off from anything that disrupts the narrow clichés of her life. Notice the walls themselves are bare and drab; they could almost be those of a female prison cell.

Brack was concerned with creating layers of meaning in his paintings and, when I think about this idea of entrapment and bondage, I can't help but surmise that the artist was also commenting upon Humphries' relationship with the character of Mrs Everage. In some ways, Humphries seems trapped inside his disguise: the clothes are a little too big for him; his hands barely fill the enormous pink gloves; the matching pink cat's-eye glasses – so unmistakably suburban and feminine – are the lenses through which he is forced to gaze, viewing the world through Edna's eyes. There is something monstrous about the housewife from Moonee Ponds, the large, claw-like hands, the exaggerated bulk of the body, and her wicked, vampirish smile. It's as if Mrs Everage is Humphries' Frankensteinian monster, a creature created from his talent and imagination, who has assumed an independent life of her own and has begun to overpower the man who made her. In this sense, Mrs Everage begins to impersonate Barry Humphries, and judging by the expression on her face, she seems elated by the fact that she has – so to speak – put little Barry in his place, back in the suburban captivity from which he fled as a child.

Successful portraits reflect the intimacy that exists between the artist and the model – so much so that the subject and the painter create the portrait together. In a landscape or a still life, no such relationship exists: a piece of fruit does not compose itself for a painting, does not participate in the angle at, or the light in which, it will be viewed by the artist. Portraiture is a conspiracy between the painter and the painted. The composer composes upon the composed. Humphries no doubt selected this particular gaudy ensemble – perhaps with the help of Brack – out of Mrs Everage's voluminous wardrobe. Humphries also composed this particular gaze from the many subtle expressions his face could assume. And his gaze is directed unswervingly back at the artist he chose to represent Edna – it's as if the three of them are immersed in some fabulous joke, in the irony of the situation. Not only is Brack composing upon the composed – the artist and the entertainer take this notion one step further, and Brack finds himself composing upon yet another composer who is composing the character of Edna Everage. The ironic twist is that this painting can also be viewed as Edna's portrait of the artist John Brack. Both painter and subject are united in their attempt to celebrate the ironies of artifice.

And what did Humphries himself think of the completed portrait? He was probably the only one of Brack's many subjects who absolutely adored the finished product. 'I think the portrait captures Edna's predatory look so well … and the shark-like smile.'

I don't what know Edna thought of the finished product. Probably, like most of Brack's sitters, she would have been appalled. Two other disgruntled subjects, who commissioned him to paint their portraits, were so devastated by Brack's interpretation of themselves that they eventually destroyed the works. In response Brack remarked, in his inimitable style, 'I do believe people get the face they deserve'.

Letter to a Young Novelist

(2004)

Inspiration

When I was a child, writing came easily. It was like an appetite that welled up through me, demanding to be sated. As rhyming couplets winged through my mind, I remember my nerves quivering, my heart racing. The only other experience that came close, years later, was when I tap danced for hours to the point of exhaustion.

From age six I filled notebooks and journals with fairytales, poems, short stories, an unfinished novel. Through my teens I sewed and bound the books with cloth, and within them mimicked my favourite writers: Oscar Wilde, Judith Wright – all of it quite dreadful, of course. At twenty, when I was on the road, busking with my father in the US, I sometimes posted twelve-page letters home, but I was unable to sustain a regular habit of writing until I began studying at Indiana University at the age of twenty-five.

The first and best lesson I learned was from an Italian–American novelist who taught a class entitled 'The Art of Fiction'. He told me not to wait around for that elliptical force – Inspiration – but to commit myself to a routine, a creative timetable, and never waver from it. At first, I was appalled: he made that divine thing called Writing seem as mundane as doing daily housework or grocery shopping. 'But what if you're in a different mood from one day to the next?' I wailed. 'Won't the tone go up and down?' 'Of course it will!' he wailed back. 'But at least you'll finish your story. And then you can read back over it and find out which tone is the best'.

I stole away from his office, still grumbling and unconvinced. The next day, however, I grudgingly did as I was instructed. I knew I worked best as soon as I woke up, and committed myself to writing three mornings a week in two-hour blocks. In bed with a cup of tea and wearing my pyjamas, I worked in longhand in a spiral-topped notebook. At first, it was difficult to concentrate for longer than two hours at a time: my mind wandered; sometimes I grew confused; other times frustrated or just plain bored. It took a few days before I began to see the point: by the end of the week I had almost finished a first draft of a short story – a *real* short story, that is – not one of the amorphous rambles I'd produced throughout my childhood.

The pages added up. As I grew accustomed to the routine, getting started in the morning was less challenging. Gradually, it became as automatic as drinking a cup of tea, or going to the bathroom. I felt my stamina growing, like a muscle. Two-hour writing sessions lengthened to three; instead of three times a week, I wrote four mornings, sometimes five, when my university classes permitted the time. I felt like an athlete in training; sometimes it reminded me of when I'd been a dancer, practising my technique each day, over and over. Of course, there were some days when I struggled to write a single good sentence. Yet there were others during which the words and images came so easily they seemed to have been delivered to me, and I experienced once again the creative thrill of my early childhood. I had enough of those effortlessly productive days – perhaps one in ten – to sustain me through the more difficult ones, and, as my teacher predicted, through the process of successive drafts the tone of the manuscript became more consistent. I fell into a pattern during which I wrote and revised one chapter of a novel a month. Nine months after I committed myself to this routine I had a manuscript, which became my first published novel, *Mood Indigo*. There are still days when I find it very hard, when I'm distracted or depressed or just plain stuck – there always will be – but I've found the odds of the routine do indeed pay good dividends and still often deliver that heightened sense of exhilaration that I experienced at the age of six.

Habits

Proust did it in bed; Nabokov did it in the bathroom; Jane Austen on the dining room table. Flaubert did it long into the night; Faulkner in the mornings; Kerouac went at it continuously for days. Very early on, the same university writing teacher told me it was important to discover the place and time that was best for me to write as an individual, to create my own rhythms and stick to them. I also found that particular accoutrements were helpful: certain pens and notebooks, a shade of ink of which I was fond, a special chair, a certain desk. The main point, I realised, was to make myself as comfortable as possible, so there were no distractions or irritations.

Most authors develop individual habits to cope with the challenges of creating something out of nothing every day – some that are productive, others that are helpful only for a short while before taking their toll. Some writers drink alcohol in order to *stop* writing, to silence the characters nattering away inside their heads, or to hush that part of the brain that is still trying to solve some narrative puzzle. It's easy to get drawn in to the numbing effects of booze and/or drugs, especially when you spend all day with a group of people who don't exist, except on the computer screen and inside your own head. When I was writing my most recent novel, I calculated that I spent about seven hours a day keeping company with my main character – twice as long as the time I spent each day with the man I was about to marry.

Writing consistently each day is not only mentally exhausting, it is also physically demanding. Norman Mailer likened the process to that of a professional sportsperson. Even western medicine now admits that the body and the mind are not separate entities; each affects and is defined by the other. It's been proven that if a university student engages in exercise after a study session, his brain will retain the information more effectively, and he'll have greater recall when he takes an exam. I find similar benefits myself when I work out directly after a long writing session. Spending hours at my desk makes me stiff and lethargic, both physically and mentally, but when I take a break and go on a strenuous walk, or lift weights at the gym, the exercise not only invigorates my body and mind, it also allows me to solve narrative problems without thinking about them directly. Many authors have similar rituals, whether they be kick-boxing, yoga or meditation.

I once had a writer friend in California who practised one day of silence once a week. For twenty-four hours, she would not speak, or experience any language at all: no conversation, television, radio, film, telephone, books, newspapers. She was convinced the absence of language for that one day stimulated her work for the rest of the week. If this suggestion seems a little New Age, I should point out that I recently unearthed a book from my library, *Becoming a Writer*, by Dorothea Brande, first published in 1934. In it, she encourages budding authors to 'induce the artistic coma' through 'wordless recreation':

> If you want to stimulate yourself into writing, amuse yourself
> in wordless ways. Instead of going to the theatre, hear a
> symphony orchestra, or go by yourself to a museum; go alone
> for long walks, or ride by yourself on a bus-top. If you will
> conscientiously refuse to talk or read you will find yourself
> compensating for it to your great advantage.

Short breaks during extended writing sessions are also a good idea, especially if you're working on a computer. If I find myself stuck during a passage, I usually jump up and stretch, or put some music on and dance around my study. More often, however, I'll perform some mindless physical task around my apartment: doing the dishes, perhaps, or sweeping the floor for five or ten minutes. By the time I go back to work my mind usually feels refreshed.

Making a Living

It usually takes a long time to be able to make a living from one's art, and so it should. There's a theory in the world of professional dance that ten years of training are required in order to even begin to move well and originally. In India, student dancers are not permitted to perform in public until they have studied the art for twenty years. In the west, a classical musician may study between ten and twenty years before securing a job in a symphony orchestra. And why should it be any different for writers?

Many assume that writing is simple because we use words every day and are frequently required either to jot things down on a piece of paper or to type a letter or a memo into a computer. Typing gets confused with writing and it's easy to think that if you have enough words on enough pages you're ready for a publishing contract and an advance.

Occasionally, in the current publishing climate, it does happen: a first-time (usually young) novelist secures a ridiculously high six-figure advance, which invariably produces outrage and envy in the quieter, older peers who have been swatting away at their craft for years. But it's important to remember that such pre-publication acclaim and hype is an excruciating burden for an author who is only just beginning. Norman Mailer has confessed that it was only after the publication of his three early novels that he began to discover his metier. The same could be said of Faulkner, Chekhov and Hemingway. Of course, the honing of an authentic literary voice does not necessarily equal commercial success and freedom from financial worries – often it's quite the reverse. But the traditional period of apprenticeship for any writer is now being collapsed – even eradicated – in the contemporary literary climate. And the people who suffer the most are not the ones who toil away, book after book, on meagre advances and scant recognition, but the 22-year-old with half a million dollars in the bank, living in a cyclone of publicity, who finds they are unable to write another word. Or the first-time author who is paraded across the world, touted by their publisher as the new Don DeLillo, only to find, six months later, that the reviews of their book are mediocre, the sales are poor, and half of the first print run has been returned to the warehouse for pulping. The press stops calling, and so does the disappointed publisher, who has lost badly on their investment. The literary agent can't get another publishing house interested in a second manuscript. And so the budding author's career is virtually over before it had a chance to sprout, let alone mature. When I was in the US a few years ago, I heard of several young first-time novelists who, knowing their literary stock had plummeted, changed their names and family backgrounds, and began resubmitting their second manuscripts as first books, pretending to be entirely 'new' authors, ready to be (re) 'discovered'.

Huge advances notwithstanding, even when an author gets their first book into print, or their second, or even third, there will probably not be enough money from royalties even to live cheaply and humbly. Some people marry wealthy partners; others live off inheritances, but most of us – if we want to keep writing and eating – will need to be creative not only on the page, but also in our lives. The ones who succeed usually choose paying work that doesn't drain their imaginations or attention too much. Maxine Hong Kingston once told me that she wrote an early draft of her acclaimed novel *The Woman Warrior* while working as a university secretary over the summer months. The job was fairly undemanding and, when she didn't have to type the odd letter or report, she'd whip out her manuscript and work on it. William Carlos Williams, who practised medicine, wrote poetry between consultations with patients. American poet Richard Hugo scribbled between shifts in an aircraft factory. Almost any successful writer can tell such stories. Some take night jobs so that their mornings are fresh and free for writing. Others work part-time. Another kind of author accepts a lucrative three-month job in an Alaskan canning factory, earning enough money to live modestly for the other nine months of the year, during which they do nothing else but their own work.

As the old adage goes: it doesn't matter how much money you make, it's how much you spend. Jonathan Franzen is a case in point: during the seven years he was writing his novel *The Corrections*, he and his wife only dined in a restaurant once a year, on the anniversary of their wedding. I know of one Australian author who has managed, with careful budgeting, to make a twelve-month Literature Board Fellowship stretch out over a second year. Then there are the writers who choose not to have children for fear of the financial strain. And if you think these are harsh sacrifices, then you should probably give up writing, because any one of the above authors would tell you that their greatest happiness is experienced when they're able to write uninterrupted each day.

A word of caution: there is the temptation for the writer with a higher degree to go into full-time academic teaching, in the belief that a university environment will be conducive to the creative life: one is surrounded by books and like-minded intellectuals; there are frequent holidays; every several years one is awarded a six-month or year-long sabbatical. But full-time teaching, even of creative writing, can become a trap. Most English departments can claim to have killed off at least one promising novelist: not only is the author/teacher swamped weekly with student writing that demands a lot of attention, their time and energy are further diminished by dreary administration duties, committee meetings, class planning, private consultations and the inevitable competitiveness and political infighting on which academia thrives. Suddenly, the creative artist is more occupied with securing a promotion to Associate Professor than with completing their second novel. A tenured teaching position does not invite any risk-taking, personal or professional. Of course, there are exceptions: Nabokov, for example, lectured at Cornell University for many years, but it didn't prevent him from having the guts or the time to write *Lolita*. These days, however, most people who manage to combine writing and academia successfully are those who teach part-time or casually: Peter Carey, for example, and the late Phillip Roth and Angela Carter.

Reviews, Publicity and Other Demons

There's an old saying: 'A portrait is never finished, only abandoned.' The same could be said of a novel, or a collection of stories. But after I've completed the final changes on my page proofs I lose interest in the work. Once the book is 'abandoned' to the public I feel as if I no longer have a relationship with it, because the story and characters have, to coin a phrase, become 'set in stone'. The manuscript and I have essentially 'divorced', and it moves on to have another relationship – a happy or unhappy one – with the reader.

There's usually about a twelve-month lead time between a book being accepted for publication and its eventual release. Like many authors, I always begin a new manuscript during that period, before too much time elapses. Diving into a new relationship with a new book serves several purposes: it softens the 'post-natal depression' that often plagues writers upon the completion of a work; it prevents an author obsessing about the public reception of his book; and it helps keep the author's prose-writing 'hand' in – as the jazz musicians say, it maintains their 'chops'.

Most contemporary publishing contracts require authors to do the publicity rounds once the book has been printed and hits the shelves. I've found most interviewers – who would have glanced at the publicity release, but not read the book – will ask me why I wrote the work in the first place. By that time, I'm usually so far into a new manuscript I find it difficult to answer. Personally, I always consider this a good sign – it means I'm enjoying the process of writing more than the product.

When my first manuscript won the Vogel Award in 1989 I was happy that it would be published, but I found myself unprepared for the publicity I was obliged to participate in. I was shy, withdrawn and tongue-tied. To put things in context, only two years before I had been supporting myself and my first husband by tap dancing at night on the streets of Kings Cross, unable to rent a cheap apartment because landlords and agents considered me a financial risk. Suddenly, journalists now wanted my opinions on any number of subjects ranging from the state of contemporary American literature to what should be done with runaway children. I was nudged in front of newspaper cameras by a well-meaning publicist. I did fourteen consecutive telephone interviews in a single afternoon. Unused to such attention, and painfully self-conscious, I strained to speak in complete sentences, to make vaguely intelligent comments, and not say, *Oh* and *Um* too much. At an interview with a journalist at an expensive Chinese restaurant I stammered a lot and kept dropping my chopsticks on the floor. The truth was, I didn't feel I had anything remarkable to say, though since these people were going to an awful lot of trouble to record and quote me, I realised I had better make sure I could invent a sage opinion or remark to make their time and effort worthwhile.

This extra pressure to be articulate and perceptive made the situation even worse. Eventually, I developed laryngitis and lost my voice altogether, which excused me from further interviews. As soon as I boarded the plane to return to the US and my university studies, I felt like a drink, and when I opened my mouth to ask for one – surprise, surprise – my voice was suddenly back, clearer than ever.

I didn't conquer this fear and dread of interviews until two books later. A close friend counselled me through the process. 'Pretend the interviewer is just a person you're meeting for the first time at a party or a dinner. Just be yourself and talk to them like you're socialising.' The advice helped; I calmed myself down beforehand, greeted the interviewer at the door, as I would a guest. I found the more I unwound and enjoyed myself, the more the journalists did, too.

There's nothing more excruciating than reading the first reviews of your new book. The muscles tense, the heart races – and that's when the review is positive. Some authors, like John Birmingham, refuse to read reviews, sparing themselves the humiliation (or joy) of public critical scrutiny. These days, a glowing review in a major national newspaper does not guarantee a jump in sales; in fact, recent figures prove that positive reviews have little effect on buying patterns. A publisher recently told me it is only a damning review in *The Age*'s literary pages that can effectively 'kill' a book in Australia.

One of the biggest problems with contemporary reviewing is that some journalists and critics are tempted to review the author rather than the book. These days, I often come away from reading a review knowing more about a novelist's agent, their advance, where they went to university, to whom they've been married, who they're fucking now, and how they cook pasta, than anything about the novel's narrative technique or structure. Often, it's obvious the reviewer has taken a dislike to the publicity sheet or the biographical material that accompanies the novel and, because it takes less time to read this material than the book, they turn what little critical skills they possess to parroting the marketing blurb sarcastically.

Time has proven that many critics of the day usually get it wrong, anyway.

Stamina

When I was visiting the US last year, a novelist friend asked me if I had ever thought: 'If this next book doesn't fly, I'm going to give up writing.' He and I had been in graduate school in the mid-'90s; he'd gone on to write two novels, published by small houses, that were moderately successful – good reviews, but sales that did not quite meet the marketing department's expectations. He was now completing a final draft of what he hoped would be his 'Big' book, the one that would break him into the literary marketplace and secure him tenure at the Midwestern university at which he taught. I could see his face was becoming lined with anxiety and anticipation. The 'Big' book had taken him four years to write; six years had been invested in the former two novels. His marriage had unravelled because he couldn't balance writing and a wife within the one life. His future was riding on the public reception of this one piece of fiction. No doubt he was hoping the 'Big' book would justify the time and personal sacrifices he'd thus far made for his work.

We've all heard stories of unpublished authors struggling to get their first books into print, the rounds of rejection letters from agents and publishers, the hopeful who submitted their work to twenty-three houses before one particular editor discovered their manuscript in the slush pile and recognised its potential. But lately, I've been hearing experiences about another kind of struggle: authors like my friend, who have published two or three books, but who have yet to enjoy the kind of critical or commercial prominence of writers they can't help but compare themselves with, writers whom they deem more 'successful'.

Sure, writing well is always challenging. Upon publication of a first book, most authors are simply thrilled and relieved to have something in print. It's a pleasure to see the volume displayed on the shelves of bookstores, or in the hands of a stranger on a bus. The struggle of writing didn't seem so hard, after all, and the effort of composing, revision, manuscript submission and repeated rejection seems to have been worth it, after all. But, as the cliché has it, the next novel is always the hardest to write. It's not called 'the curse of the second book' for nothing. The author privately suspects they have only one book in them and their task now becomes one of proving to themselves and to the public that they are capable of constructing something more complex than a lightly fictionalised autobiography of their childhood, or the story of their first marriage with the names changed. Due to this kind of self-imposed pressure many bad second novels are written – they're often strained, overblown or struggling to be different. The ease and lightness with which the first one was written is gone, and in trundles a book heavy with self-conscious symbolism and clever allusions, a novel with which the author's publishers hope to announce to the world their breadth of 'range'. Instead, it is mildly praised by reviewers, short-listed for one of the state literary awards, and sells 1500 copies. The book and the author are promptly forgotten. Unless, that is, the writer has the need and the courage to start yet another novel and begin from scratch again.

And this is the point at which my friend now finds himself – if this third one doesn't 'do it', he'll probably throw in the towel, become a full-time book reviewer or an editor himself, or teach writing to undergraduates in rural colleges until his retirement. Yet it isn't for lack of talent or discipline that he finds himself in this position. All that has happened is that he has allowed a mercurial force like public opinion to corrupt the private relationship he'd formerly had with his own work.

Once this has occurred, it's easy for a writer to lose faith in his own voice and originality, to be tempted into producing a kind of literary shopping list, to strike a bargain between his imagination and the marketplace. If novels based on Australian historical myths are selling well overseas, the hapless author begins a 'fictional autobiography' of Henry Lawson, or a 'contemporary fable' about the bunyip; 'concept' books are all the rage and suddenly our author is writing a novel based on the history of the rotary clothes line; magic realism goes down well with the critics: throw in a few angels and a dog that levitates. Simone de Beauvoir once commented that she wrote books in order to be loved. I think there are easy ways to garner affection, but writing isn't one of them.

I could make a long list of authors who were damned by the public when they published their best work: Joyce, Flaubert, Whitman, (Mary) Shelley, Nabokov, Behn, to name a few. But what writer wouldn't want to produce a book that would in time make a mark as strong as *Ulysses*? Nabokov won only one major literary prize – the National Book Award – during his American career; Proust didn't win anything significant; neither did Joyce. I think the one thing the above writers had in common was that they were quite willing to risk not being loved. In fact, they were prepared to allow their books to be misunderstood or even loathed by the critics and readers of the time. I don't see this kind of defiance much anymore. Too many authors are straining for acceptance, like a line of eager debutantes dressed up at a society ball, hoping their dance cards will be filled by the end of the night.

When William Faulkner published what is considered to be one of his greatest novels, *The Sound and the Fury*, in 1929, it barely sold out its first print run of 1700 copies over an eighteen-month period. At the same time, he struggled to make a living from publishing short stories in commercial magazines such as *Scribner's* and the *Saturday Evening Post*. Of the thirty-seven submissions he made in a single year, only six were accepted. Unable to support himself by writing fiction, he reluctantly worked as a screenwriter in Hollywood for MGM and 20th Century Fox. Only a few years before he won the Nobel Prize for Literature in 1950, all but one of his novels were out of print.

In 1940, when Christina Stead published what she considered to be her 'best book to date', *The Man Who Loved Children*, it sold so slowly at the price of $2.75 that it had to be reduced to $1.75 to sell out its print run of 5000 copies. This was at a time when there was no television, no video, no DVDs, no internet to rival the attention of potential readers. The reviews of the book varied from scathing to lukewarm: Mary McCarthy, writing for the *New Republic*, thought it was 'peculiar, breathless, overwritten and incoherent' and likened it to an 'hysterical tirade'. The Australian reviews were slightly better, although patronising. An anonymous reviewer writing for the *Sydney Morning Herald* praised her for finally adopting a conventional novelistic form, for modifying her 'rich and strange mode of expression'. It wasn't until twenty-five years later, when the novel was republished by Holt, Rinehart and Winston at the insistence of poet Randall Jarrell, who wrote an enthusiastic introduction, that it was recognised by Pearl Bell as 'one of the superb novels of the twentieth Century'.

When I first met Louis Nowra several years ago, he told me an interesting story. In 1985, he had his eighth play, *The Golden Age*, produced at the Playbox Theatre. The work was pilloried by every Melbourne theatre critic, and subsequent productions throughout Australia in the mid-'80s attracted a similar critical response. Needless to say, the play was a dismal commercial flop as well, with near-empty houses and very short runs. Even though he was pleased by what he had achieved with the realisation of the play, he was so shaken by the public response to what he considered to be his best theatrical work that he stopped writing plays for three years and planned to go back to university to become a mycologist. It's very hard for an author to resist making this classic mistake: he had assumed that the critics of the time 'knew' more than he did. (In fact, there have since been university theses written entirely about the initial negative critical responses to the play.) Nineteen years later, *The Golden Age* is not only considered an Australian classic (frequent professional and amateur productions in Australia and internationally; on the HSC and many university reading lists), it also makes the author a considerable amount of money each year.

Of course, there are many books and plays that deserve the bad reviews they receive, but the point to remember is that no one knows your work better than you do, and if you have devoted yourself to the making of it sincerely, if your vision equals your execution, if you know you've completed the book you intended to write, then sometimes that has to be reward enough. Naturally, the responses of close writing peers are invaluable, because writers usually read differently from the general public, and one appreciates their opinions more than anyone else's – particularly when, during a final draft, they recognise one's narrative intentions and suggest ways in which they might be achieved. I've always had two or three close writing friends in my life, whose opinions I trust, who give mercilessly honest feedback on my final drafts.

Frequently I think the so-called writer's block is not due to a lack of imagination, but a lack of isolation. I'm not just talking about geography – the proverbial 'room of one's own' – I'm also referring to a necessary psychological distance from the machinations of the literary world. I wouldn't go as far as JD Salinger – to a remote country property filled with safes that hold manuscripts only to be published after his death – but I do admire the impulse. A calculated withdrawal from popular opinion allows space and time for more private, personal preoccupations, the most important of which is the writer's work, and the relationship they continue to develop with it.

There are many ways in which authors can cultivate this kind of distance. One is to stop reading book reviews altogether. Another is to stop reading contemporary literature and concentrate on good books from other eras. Yet another is to resist the temptation to discuss the book you're currently working on with friends and acquaintances, let alone allowing them to read it – not until the final draft, anyway. I think Ben Okri had the right idea when he said: 'There is no genuine creative or human problem that cannot be solved if you are serene enough, humble enough, hardworking enough …' It's easier to be serene, humble and hardworking when you're somewhat detached from the expectations of the public.

During the several years Flaubert was writing *Madame Bovary* he lived with his mother, sister-in-law and niece in provincial Rouen. His Parisian lover, Louise Colet, and his several close friends frequently tried to persuade him to move to Paris and take up 'his position in literary society'. Since he worked on his manuscript each day from one o'clock in the afternoon until one in the morning, he argued that he could hardly find the time to assume such a position. He refused to move to Paris and publish prematurely and, by doing that, he also refused to enter the usual literary bun fights that can often distract authors from regular, hard work. When he was only thirty-one he wrote to Maxime Du Camp:

> 'To be known' is not my chief concern: that can give complete gratification only to very mediocre vanities. Besides, is there ever any certainty about this? ... seldom does anyone but a fool die sure of his own reputation. Fame, therefore, can no more serve you as a gauge of your own worth than obscurity.

Flaubert certainly benefited from being obscure to the public and its popular opinion, and the public (eventually) benefited from the obscurity in which his novel was written. But did Flaubert know, in 1852, that he was writing his 'Big' book? Yes, he did. Would he have given up writing if, upon publication, *Madame Bovary* had failed to attract attention? I certainly doubt it. The poet Richard Hugo went so far as to believe that accolades and attention are an anathema to the creative process, and that we should all 'hope hard to fall always short of success'. Maybe some of us don't have to hope that hard, but I think the gig for all is to be able to stand back from popular and critical opinion, from the pressure from publishers to produce the next book, from sales figures and literary awards, and remember the almost sensuous pleasure of when we're sitting alone in a room and writing well.

Shaun Prescott: Modern Misfit

(2018)

When I finished reading Shaun Prescott's debut novel, *The Town*, I was keen to know more about the author, whose biography is unusually brief: he lives in the Blue Mountains and has had a few short pieces previously published in literary magazines. In an era obsessed by relentless self-promotion, I was surprised to discover that Prescott has no website, no Instagram account, no Facebook author page. And he has no media profile. *The Town* is such an original and commanding debut that I wondered if it had been written by a much older and more experienced author impersonating a younger one – or if Prescott, like Thomas Pynchon, was deliberately marketing himself as a recluse.

As I finish telling this story to Prescott, thirty-three, and his partner, Rachel, they both break into laughter. We're sitting in the backyard of their Katoomba cottage with their inquisitive kids, Edith, three, and Darcy, eighteen months.

Amused, Prescott replies, 'No, there was no attempt to be anonymous'.

'He's got a Twitter account!' Rachel offers, as she bounces the baby on her hip.

The Town was published late last year by not-for-profit Melbourne publisher Brow Books, and has received resoundingly positive reviews. However, when Brow editor Sam Cooney suggested that they try to secure publication of the novel overseas, Prescott replied, 'Don't bother. No one'll like it. It's too Australian'.

Prescott was proved wrong when the rights to *The Town* sold immediately into multiple territories at the 2017 Frankfurt book fair: Faber & Faber in the UK; Farrar, Straus & Giroux in the US; Buchet/Chastel at Libella in France; Blumenbar at Aufbau in Germany; and Literatura Random House in Spain. Faber has championed the book as 'a stunning modern reincarnation of the existential novel'. It's an extraordinary achievement for both a small, non-profit Australian press and a first-time author. 'I still think they're going to ring me up and tell me it's all off', admits Prescott. Originally, Prescott had planned to self-publish the book.

The Town's greatest achievement is a perfect confluence of voice, tone and subject matter. The premise of the novel is that the narrator lives in a small town of Central NSW, and is writing a novel about the disappearing towns of Central NSW. He introduces realistic characters in a realistic setting, but they are all trapped in unthinking, repetitive behaviour, whether it's the host of a regular radio show that has no listeners; a bus driver who sticks rigidly to his route and timetable, even though it's been years since anyone has boarded his vehicle; and a hotel publican who opens her pub every day in spite of the fact she attracts no customers. And then, as the narrator continues to write his novel about the disappearing towns, life begins to imitate art and the town he's living in slowly begins to vanish.

'I've been writing since I was a kid', says Prescott, lifting Edith onto his lap. 'I used to fill up exercise books, and my mother encouraged me'. I suggest that only someone who has grown up in a small Australian town could have written a novel such as *The Town*.

'I grew up in Manildra', he confesses. 'From the age of five to nineteen. It's in the Central West of NSW. It's a flour-mill town'.

'And your father worked in the flour mill?'

He nods. 'Yeah, for a few years'.

Rachel, possibly sensing her partner's shyness, jumps in to tell a story: 'One day (children's author) Jackie French came to the school to give a talk. And afterwards, his mother gave her these stories that Shaun had written'.

'Did she give him any feedback?'

Rachel nods. 'For about six years! God, she was a brutal critic—'

An embarrassed Shaun shakes his head. 'No, she was right be brutal ... She gave me great feedback'.

Rachel adds, 'As a kid he was a real people-watcher. His mother told me that. He was always sitting back and observing people'.

Prescott did not come from a bookish family, though his grandfather once gave him a box of ageing genre fiction, which he quickly devoured. He has never studied literature, nor taken a creative writing class. His one concession to a formal education, at the insistence of his uncle, was studying for a journalism degree at Bathurst University. 'He knew that writing for a living was pretty hard, and that I might need something to fall back on'.

It was during his first year at university that he read his first literary novel. '*White Noise*, by Don DeLillo', he says. The works of authors such as Franz Kafka, Robert Walser and Thomas Bernhard followed. 'Anything not naturalistic'.

The experiences at university were vital to Prescott in another way. The town portrayed in his novel is vivid and utterly familiar – yet remains unnamed throughout the narrative. 'The actual grid of the (fictional) town is based on Bathurst', he says. 'I returned there during the writing of the book to achieve clarity'.

Throughout his life, Prescott has started many novels, but up until now has never finished them. 'I tend to work in spurts', he says.

As his daughter slips off his lap, he admits, 'Edith gave me the discipline to write seriously. By the time she was born, I was over socialising and going out all the time'. I have to admit, I've already fallen a little bit in love with Edith, who has scrawled lines and patterns all over her bare legs with a variety of texta colours. She's nicknamed me 'Bambi', and has earlier boasted that she is 'also a writer'.

Prescott explains that he wrote the book at night, on the balcony of his former Marrickville home, after his daughter went to sleep. 'I wrote the first four chapters in a rush over four nights. After that, I didn't write it chronologically'.

'How did you know that this was the novel that had legs?'

Prescott shrugs. 'I didn't know it had legs. I didn't know where it was going'.

This is the kind of writing process I find most scary. I call it 'writing without a net', without any unfolding sense of plot or structure. The thought of doing it myself makes my skin crawl, though plenty of great writers have chosen – and still choose – this method of composition.

Instead, Prescott tells me, he intuited 'when things needed to change' in the story by repeatedly re-reading what he'd previously written.

'I just don't know if I could have written it if it were heavily plotted'. He takes baby Darcy from Rachel and settles him on his knee. 'I wrote it without any expectation that it would be published – it was purely for the pleasure of writing'.

All this time, Edith has been playing nearby, eavesdropping on the conversation. Suddenly she turns to me, and demands, 'Why are you talking about Daddy?' as if he's the most boring person in the world.

After we stop laughing, Sean clarifies why writing *The Town* was different from his earlier attempts. 'The reason I could finish the book is because I figured the voice out. It was a voice close to my own'.

Rachel agrees. 'Friends say they can hear your voice in it'.

'I've also noticed', I remark, 'that the narrative doesn't have any metaphorical language in it. But then again, it works so well, because the whole book is a metaphor'.

Prescott frowns and nods. 'I'm not very good at pulling off metaphorical flourishes', he admits. 'Everyday language, to me, is sonically appealing'. Here, his background as a guitarist and music critic is obvious, which also surfaces in the rhythms and repetitions of *The Town*.

What is not appealing to Prescott is elliptical storytelling. 'I can't stand a lot of space on the page. You know, a line here. A word there. Tiny bits of dialogue all the way down the margin'. He makes a face, as if the baby just farted.

'I like walls of text', he continues. 'Because inside that text there is music. I wanted it (the novel) to be walls of text. That density keeps holding you in'.

'In what draft did the town begin to disappear? The first or the second?'

'Oh, the town was always going to disappear', he says, confidently.

Though Prescott has a study inside the cottage, he still prefers to write at night on the covered back porch, after his daughter has gone to bed, using an old dented cake tin as an ashtray. Then he is up at 5.30am to make the two-hour train commute to the city for his job writing for a magazine and website that features video games and new technologies.

Would he ever like to be in the position where he could write full-time?

He shudders at the thought. 'As you know, most of writing is a process of things not going well. (So) if it's the only thing going on, and it's not going well, then—'

I turn to Rachel: 'Can you tell when his writing is not going well?'

She grins. 'Yes, I can tell. He'll come to bed cranky'.

The couple met ten years ago in Marrickville through mutual friends. Their romance blossomed over $2.50 beers and $5 meals at The Taverners Hill Hotel, '—which we bought with coupons from the local supermarket', Rachel adds, laughing. A teacher of literature, she is Prescott's first reader. 'But he only gives me things to read in bits. I can't see all the chapters in order, not until he finishes it'.

The family is so close, the four members seem like extensions of the one being. Edith takes my hand and herds us all in to the house, where she shows me a scrapbook filled with what looks like graffiti written in Mandarin.

Later, Shaun leads me into his study and shows me a collection of local history books about small Australian towns. One is about Manildra, the flour-mill town in which he grew up. He points to an item at the bottom of a page, and I recognise it as a scene re-created in the book.

'The locals had a competition to see who could throw a dog over the roof of the pub'. He grins and shakes his head. 'How could I not use that?'

On another page is a primary school photo of Prescott's sixth-grade class, and I glimpse a steely-eyed boy sitting on a bench, gazing out in to a small Australian town that he would one day mythologise into a quiet masterpiece.

CODA

LIFE

People Power at Ponderosa

First published in SBS Online, 16 May 2017, Ben Naparstek (ed.).

Following the publication of this essay, Housing NSW was publicly shamed into finally renovating Theo's mouldy apartment. Theo was so thrilled by the transformation that when he suffered a recent heart attack, he refused to be taken by ambulance to hospital because he was enjoying his home too much. A few months later Junkie John died of an overdose.

As this book was going to print, Theo passed away peacefully in his sleep, in his apartment at Ponderosa, on 14 June 2018.

Wild Frontier: The Child Gangs of Tweed Heads

First published in *The Monthly*, March 2010, Ben Naparstek (ed.).

Shortly after this essay was published I received an abusive letter from the gang members' grandmother, defending her 'good boys', and questioning the claims of the many victims, whom she dismissed as alcoholics. The essay was one of three pieces shortlisted for the 2011 Walkley Awards for Best Longform Journalism.

The Hordes

First published under the title 'Staying Power' in the *Good Weekend*, 13 April 2013, Ben Naparstek (ed.).

Today, my cousins continue to live in the East Malvern house, cramped by all the clutter and possessions that they cannot bear to relinquish. I still send them Christmas cards every year, and I am told they have kept every one of them.

The Tincture of Health

First published in *The Monthly*, April 2010, Ben Naparstek (ed.).

In 2013, Tony Bower was arrested at his property for cultivating 200 marijuana plants he'd planned to convert into tinctures. He was sentenced to twelve months in jail, but upon appeal was released after six weeks on a twelve-month good behaviour bond. Naturally, the bond forbade him from cultivating any more marijuana or treating his many patients.

Flying High: The Rise and Guise of Self-Funded Retirees

First published in *Griffith Review 45: The Way We Work*, 2015, Julianne Schultz (ed.).

I was fortunate to be able to interview the meth cook 'Don Miller' (real name John Griffiths) in 2015, because shortly after this article was published, John developed dementia and had to be confined to a nursing home. For a short while, before his illness developed, we were friends. Apart from being obsessed by chemistry, he developed a fixation with the animated children's film *Frozen*, which he praised constantly. He died in May 2017, leaving all his chemical formulas to his best mate, who wishes to remain anonymous.

Girls Gone Wild

First published in the *Good Weekend*, 11 July 2013, Ben Naparstek (ed.).

By the time this article was published, Leeyah had been arrested again and was in Silverwater prison. Ironically, a moody colour portrait of her, taken by James Brickwood, made the front cover of the *Good Weekend*, but in jail she had no access to newspapers. I posted her a copy, along with a short letter. After she was released she told me that she passed the magazine around to the other prisoners and the staff and immediately the article made her 'the Queen of fucking Silverwater!'

I kept in touch with Jamie and Leeyah for a couple of years. Whenever Jamie needed money she'd come up to the Cross with either her friends or her mother and, if I could afford it, I would slip her fifty bucks. In December 2012, Jamie returned the favour by comforting me just after I'd received the news of the death of my father-in-law.

I encouraged Leeyah to concentrate on her art work, which was the only activity – apart from getting high – that she enjoyed. On a stretch between prison sentences, she wanted to begin to look for work, and asked me to type up her resume, which I did.

Sadly, Leeyah's unsentimental prediction in the article, 'I think I'll end up in jail … And I think you'll be the one who'll get pregnant', proved true. While Leeyah was serving yet another stint in the lock-up, Jamie celebrated her nineteenth birthday 'by the suiside bulding' (sic) at the Waterloo Public Housing Estate, to which she invited me. There, she met a boy her age who promptly got her pregnant before returning to jail himself. Upon his release, she fell pregnant again, and they moved into Public Housing in Sydney's Western suburbs. The relationship didn't last and now Jamie is a single mother of a boy and a girl. As far as I know, Leeyah is still serving time.

Elsie Turns Forty

First published in the *Good Weekend*, 12 April 2014, Ben Naparstek (ed.).

I have kept in touch with some of the subjects who appeared in this article. I learned that Marie and her daughters did indeed escape interstate, and are now enjoying a quiet and anonymous life. Polly and her children remain safe and happy and are now living in suburban Sydney. In September 2014, the Elsie refuge was closed down by the Baird government, as were all the other refuges run for and by women in NSW, and the government launched a campaign encouraging those who'd become estranged from their families to return home. It was called 'Going Home and Staying Home', hardly an option for women and children fleeing domestic abuse. The original funds for women's refuges were reallocated to the Salvation Army.

LOVE

Love and Death in Darlinghurst

First published in the anthology *Take Me With You: Stories of Long-Distance Love*, Sarah McDonald (ed.), Random House, Sydney, 2005.

After eighteen years together, and fifteen years of marriage, Louis and I continue to live in separate apartments, but the dogs co-habit with me because they prefer my taste in music. My father's ashes are still stored inside the snare drum in a corner of the living room.

My New Orleans

First published in *The Bulletin Summer Reading Issue*, December 2005–January 2006, Ashley Hay (ed.).

Many of my ex-husband's relatives lost their homes in Hurricane Katrina, and were forced to relocate to nearby Texas, which they loathe, because the 'Crescent City' embodied so much of their African and Caribbean heritage. Since Katrina, I have been unable to return to New Orleans either, because my memories juxtaposed against the realities of the city today would probably be too traumatic.

Sleepless in Samoa

First published in the anthology *Better than Fiction* 2, Don George and Samantha Forge (eds), Lonely Planet Publications, London, 2015.

Louis did end up writing a travel article on Samoa for the *Sydney Morning Herald*. I briefly considered writing to Aggie Grey's Hotel to request the return of my bag of sex toys, but in the end I was too embarrassed.

A Writer in the Family

This essay was first published as 'Writers in the Family' in the *Weekend Australian*, 19–20 February 2005.

Louis and I did not end up having children. And fortunately our dogs remain illiterate.

For the Love of Dog

The first half of this essay, 'Coco', was first published as 'When My Furry Best Friend Got Cancer' in SBS Online, 24 February 2016. Belinda So (ed.).

It was fortunate that Louis wrote a book inspired by Basil, because the following year Basil suffered a spate of illnesses: pancreatitis; Cushing's disease; the breaking of a cruciate ligament. The royalties he received from the publication of the novel paid for Basil's astronomical vet bills. At the age of thirteen, Coco remains in rude good health.

The Gift of Life

This essay was first published as 'Can You Spare a Kidney?' in the *Good Weekend*, 5 October 2013, Ben Naparstek (ed.).

Shortly after this essay was published, Leanne Azoulas almost lost her life to chronic organ failure, and spent weeks in intensive care. Two years later, she received a life-saving transplant and now lives at home with her parents.

In 2017, public awareness of organ failure was raised by the production of the stage play *Mark Colvin's Kidney*, based on the experiences of Colvin's kidney transplant from a live donor. It was written by Tommy Murphy and produced by Belvoir St Theatre, Sydney.

In the US, human trials of a bionic kidney were due to start in late 2017. The technology is based on a microchip made by silicon nanotechnology, one similar to the microelectronics used in computers.

On 10 February 2018, my brother Jason celebrated his ten-year transplant anniversary and remains in good health. He is now married with a four-year-old son.

Goodbye, Pork Pie Hat: Fourteen Ways to Say Farewell

This essay first appeared in the anthology *My Mother, My Father: On Losing a Parent*, Susan Wyndham (ed.), Random House, Sydney, 2013.

LITERATURE AND ART

Thea Astley Comes Out of the Shadows

This essay first appeared in the *Good Weekend*, 28 September 1996, Anne Summers (ed.).

My literary agent, Jill Hickson, had negotiated the terms of my writing this profile with the editors of the *Good Weekend*. The day after the interview took place, however, Thea rang up her literary agent, also Jill Hickson, and tried to have the profile stopped. No reason was given, except that she'd changed her mind. Jill, having once been the victim of an unkind article about herself, sided with Thea and tried to talk me out of proceeding. But I'd already invested a lot of time researching and recording Thea – I also needed the money, 12 per cent of which Jill had already negotiated to collect. And anyway, why would Thea presume that I'd do a hatchet job on her? The only sane reason I could think of was that she'd confessed, off the record, that she'd once tried marijuana, but 'didn't like it', an admission that I'd already chosen not to include. When Jill and Thea insisted that they read and approve the copy before it was published, I politely refused them. Even though this was my first foray into longform journalism, I knew enough about the ethics to ignore their demands.

Fortunately, the magazine editors were supportive and sympathetic. Not only did they refuse to pull the profile, they sent me back down to Thea's place with a professional photographer, so an image could be snapped of us drinking tea and chatting. By this time, Thea was refusing to co-operate. Whenever the lens was aimed at her she'd put her head down and rest her chin against her chest, or suddenly turn away, so the photographer could only snap frames of her hair and shoulders. I felt sorry for the poor shutter-bug: he'd spent two and a half hours driving down the coast for one or two shots, and Thea was going to make sure he'd never get them. The only way he could capture the two of us together was by standing in a paddock about 50 metres away and shooting us with a telephoto lens, as if he were a paparazzo. Even then, Thea managed to bow and look down at the ground so that all that could be seen in the published image was the crown of her head.

On the morning the profile was published, Thea rang at seven, waking me up, and abused me for misspelling the German word 'Massie'. 'See, I told you I should have read it before you published it! I *knew* you'd mess something up!'

The manuscript I was struggling to complete at the time of interviewing Thea was my first memoir, *Dreamtime Alice*, which I finally finished two months later, and which was published in 1998. It won the National Biography Award in 2000.

The new manuscript Astley mentions at the end of the essay was published by Penguin in 1999, under the title *Drylands*. It won the 2000 Queensland Premier's Award for Fiction, and the 2000 Miles Franklin Award. *Drylands* was Astley's final novel before her death in 2004, and my profile on her was her final interview.

Karen Lamb's excellent biography of Astley, *Thea Astley: Inventing Her Own Weather*, was published in 2015 (UQP).

Sex, Lies and Defamation

This essay first appeared in the *Australian Literary Review*, March 2006, Stephen Romei (ed.)

I still keep in touch with Margaret Tyler. Whenever I visit her in northern NSW, we go out to lunch, and she gives me some of the vintage clothes she used to wear in the '60s.

In Ernest: Hemingway and the Art of the Story

First published in *HEAT New Series* (No 2): 'Fitzroy to Freo', 2001, Ivor Indyk (ed.).

This essay was written as part of my Doctoral thesis on the modern short story at the University of Technology, Sydney, 2002.

Satirists of Suburbia: Mrs Edna Everage Paints John Brack

First published in *Art & Australia*, Vol. 45, No. 1, Spring 2007, Eleonora Triguboff (ed.).

While writing this essay, I contacted Brack's widow, Helen Maudsley, who generously assisted me with my enquiries and recommended certain books for my research.

Letter to a Young Novelist

First published in *HEAT New Series* (No. 8): 'And So Forth', 2004, Ivor Indyk (ed.).

My university friend, who was writing his 'big book', gave up writing after his manuscript was rejected by several publishers. He has since become a literary agent.

Sources: *Becoming a Writer*, Dorothea Brande, Harcourt, Brace & Company, New York, 1934; *The Spooky Art: Some Thoughts on Writing*, Norman Mailer, Little, Brown & Company, 2003, London; *Christina Stead: A Biography*, Hazel Rowley, William Heinemann Australia, Melbourne, 1993; *Faulkner: A Biography*, Joseph Blotner, Random House, New York, 1974; *A Way of Being Free*, Ben Okri, Phoenix House, London, 1997; *The Letters of Gustave Flaubert 1830–1857*, Francis Steegmuller (ed.), Faber, London, 1979; *The Triggering Town*, Richard Hugo, WW Norton & Company, New York, 1979.

Since 2004, social media has become an almost compulsory part of any writer's life. Yes, the internet is an excellent tool for research, but a handy distraction for procrastinators. What's worse, the machine that allows us access to the web is the same one we depend on to produce our work. How easy it is to take a pause from the toil of writing prose, flip windows, and gaze at pictures of cup cakes and kittens. I know of at least one novelist who, when trying to meet a publishing deadline, moves into a hotel without wi-fi access until she's completed her latest book. Others have software installed into their computers that denies them an internet connection until a certain time in the afternoon. Still others retreat from social media altogether, shunning Twitter, Instagram and Facebook in order to better focus on their manuscripts.

It's a tough call to make, because publishers now demand that writers have at least a Facebook author page and engage with other forms of social media to promote upcoming publications and events. Some authors go so far as to record a three-minute trailer of their new novel, like those that promote feature films. The logic goes that the more presence you have on social media, the more books you sell. I've noticed, however, that Tim Winton is not on Facebook, Helen Garner doesn't use Instagram and Peter Carey has never tweeted.

Some writers even begin promoting their books before they've finished them. Many times, I've seen Facebook posts of a manuscript page, usually a first draft and crudely written. It's obvious that the author is feeling vulnerable and needs a virtual pat on the back, some admiring comments, some encouraging feedback. But the very vulnerability that authors seek to avoid is exactly what they need to complete their works. Uncertainty is the essence of creativity.

Shaun Prescott: Modern Misfit

This essay was first published as 'Perfecting a Metaphor', in the *Weekend Australian*, 10 February 2018.

Acknowledgments

Many thanks to Ben Naparstek, who, as a 23-year-old new editor of *The Monthly*, sought me out and persuaded me to attempt longform investigative journalism. Without his invitation and enthusiasm this book would not exist.

Thanks to Louis Nowra for critical feedback on these essays. And to Phillipa McGuinness for contracting them to be published in a single volume. I would also like to express my gratitude to Sophia Oravecz for her steady and sensitive project management, and to Susan McCreery for her superlative editing and proofreading skills.

www.ingramcontent.com/pod-product-compliance
Lightning Source LLC
Chambersburg PA
CBHW020058030726
47498CB00006B/1843